THE COMPLETE VEGAN BAKING COOKBOOK FOR BEGINNERS

Your go-to sweet, delicious and simple plant based recipes for any occasion with original recipes for cookies, bars, pastries, pies, cakes and more

Caterina Milano

SPECIAL BONUS!

Want this Bonus Book free?

Get **FREE**, unlimited access to it and all of my new books by joining the Fan Base!

SCAN WITH YOUR CAMERA TO JOIN!

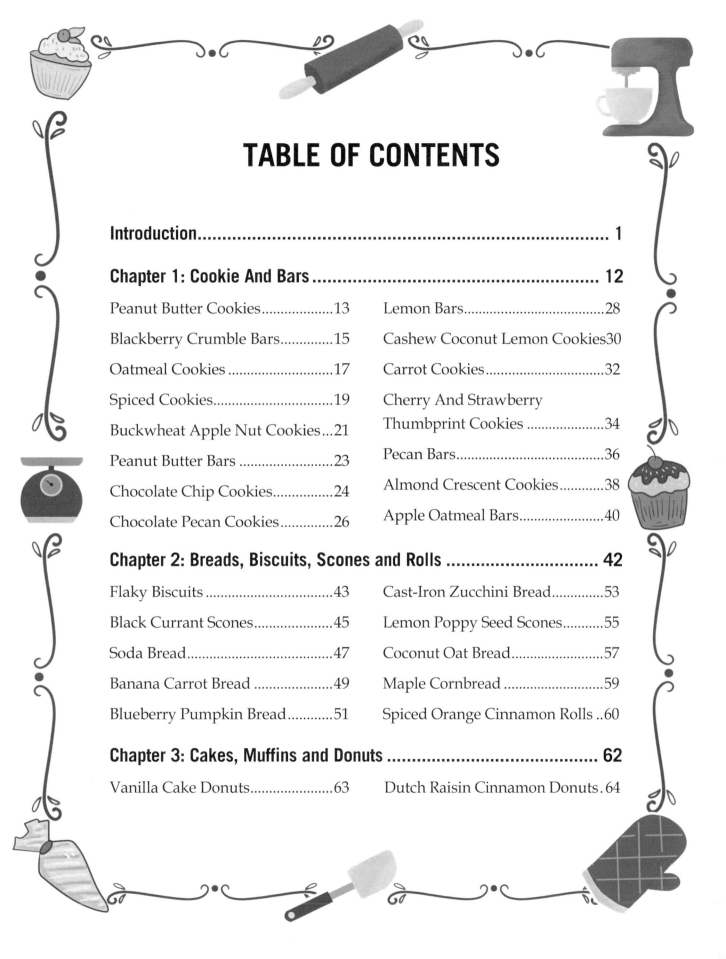

TABLE OF CONTENTS

Chapter 4: Tarts And Pies 96

Conclusion 112

INTRODUCTION

Some people have fallen prey to the false notion that vegans only eat bland, flavorless foods such as salads and vegetables. Others even believe that you have to follow a monotonous routine and eat the same food over and over again. However, just because you are eating vegan food doesn't mean there is no variety in your diet. Every non-vegan food can be made into a vegan version, including baked goods such as chocolate chip cookies and flaky biscuits. However, before we get to the baking recipes, let's talk about the basics of vegan baking.

If you are new to vegan food, it is important to remember it doesn't have to be all or nothing. Eating just one vegan meal a day will contribute to improving your overall health and also make a difference in sustaining global resources.

Why Bake Vegan?

A Forbes magazine article states that the number of consumers in America that identify as vegan grew by about 600% between 2014 and 2017. The trend of "vegan baking" follows the same statistics and has caught a lot of attention in the last decade. Avoiding animal products is one of the easiest ways to reduce the strain on the global food supply and other essential resources. Vegan baking is also known to provide multiple health benefits.

Health Benefits of Vegan Baking

It's easy to see why traditional desserts are not at all that healthy. Most of them contain trans fats and refined carbs, and lack nutrient-dense calorie content. The dairy in most desserts, like butter and cheese, is a storehouse of fat and cholesterol but has minimal nutritional value. On the contrary, vegan baking is healthier overall and is tastier too. It's a win-win for the lifestyle of today. It is 100% plant-based and completely dairy-free. In other words, vegan baking offers excellent nutritional value.

- **Vegan baking offers Unsaturated fats**

These fats lower your LDL cholesterol levels and provide the body with nutrients like omega-3 fatty acids that can reduce inflammation and rheumatism-related health risks. Unsaturated fats are found in nuts like walnuts, cashews, almonds, and peanuts. They are also found in oils like avocado, peanut, olive, soybean, sunflower and corn oil.

- **High fiber content**

Consuming a balanced amount of fiber can help to reduce the risk of chronic diseases including obesity, and diabetes. Vegan desserts containing apples, bananas, beans, oranges, pear, raspberries, strawberries, and whole grains, are high in fiber and other nutritious values.

- **Combats lactose intolerance**

Anyone who is lactose intolerant or has a dairy-free diet should try vegan desserts. They don't contain any milk, and their mouth-watering flavors and high nutritional content are irresistible.

Not only are they numerous health benefits from baking vegan, but it is also the best option for global resource sustainability as well as the welfare of animals.

Animal Welfare

With the increasing amount of cruelty against animals and their products, it has become more than necessary to contribute to veganism. An egg is a standard product used in almost every baked recipe, but what happens to the hens and the eggs before they reach your home?

Most of the industrial egg industry exploits hens by forcing molting in order to change their reproductive systems and increase profits. This practice is banned and declared illegal in the EU. The hens are starved, so the molting that is supposed to occur in the winter occurs early. Flocks grow entirely new feathers when the natural molting is exploited. This starving and forced molting damages the overall health of the hens at such commercial poultry farms. The practices that occur on dairy farms to produce cream, milk and butter are also very inhumane and yet continue in many countries.

When one shifts from non-vegan products to a plant-based diet, they also reduce the carbon footprint. Veganism is a sustainable option that helps people improve their quality of life and preserve the earth at the same time.

What is the difference between being a Vegan and a Vegetarian?

There are some essential differences between vegans and vegetarians. Vegans are known to eliminate all dairy and meat products and encourage only plant-based products. On the other hand, vegetarians stop eating any kind of food that contains meat. There are three divisions in the category of vegetarianism:

- Those who consume eggs, milk, and occasionally poultry, fish, and ham but no beef at all are known as semi-vegetarians.
- Those who drink only milk but exclude the consumption of eggs, meat, and fish are classified as lacto-vegetarians.
- Another classification of vegetarians is lacto-ovo. These allow milk and eggs but tend to eliminate fish and meat products from their diets.

The History of Vegan Baking

Veganism dates back to 500 BCE when Pythagoras, a mathematician, and a Greek philosopher, was known to promote benevolence among all species and adopted a vegetarian diet. It is believed that around the time of Budhha, the concept of vegan diets was promoted.

But it was not until 1806 that this practice started taking shape, and Dr. William Lambe and Percy Bysshe Shelley became the first Europeans to object to the use of eggs and dairy. This was mainly because of the practices followed by the breeders and for ethical reasons.

About three years after this, Rev. Sylvester Graham co-founded the American Vegetarian Society and promoted and obeyed temperance, vegetarianism, abstinence, and frequent bathing. In 1944 Donald Watson - a British woodworker, created the term "vegan" to differentiate between those who do not eat meat but consume dairy and eggs.

During this time period, tuberculosis was found in about 40% of dairy cows all over Britain. Watson made sure to use this to his advantage and claimed that veganism provides protection against tainted food.

Since then, the process of vegan baking has contributed to the vegan diet, giving people more options because of personal choices or health conditions. There is no doubt that there are many more types of food to be explored and experimented with.

The Basics Of Vegan Baking

Vegan baking can feel intimidating and a little overwhelming in the beginning since there are so many recipes and cooking methods. Nevertheless, there are some basic rules of vegan baking that determine what ingredients to use and how to prepare them. Once you understand these baking principles, you will be on your way to becoming the next great vegan baker.

Measure Your Ingredients Properly

Baking is not like cooking. It is a science. Therefore, you must measure every ingredient precisely. You should also use the same measurements for every ingredient. Do not switch from using volume to weight measurements. For the purposes of this baking cookbook, we will be using the US imperial system (with metric conversions), so you will need American measuring cups (or metric measuring devices) to precisely measure out your ingredients. In addition to this, measure your ingredients out before you begin making the recipe. I know what you're thinking; pre-measuring out the ingredients will only make more dishes to clean. However, pre-measuring the ingredients will make the mixing process flow smoothly. Can you imagine if you are making a recipe for apple pie that has a lot of ingredients? Stopping and measuring every single ingredient one by one while you are mixing the recipe will actually lengthen the preparation time. Save yourself the trouble and pre-measure the ingredients.

Follow The Recipe To A Tee

As I mentioned before, baking is a science, so you need to follow the recipe to the letter. If your recipe calls for sifting the dry ingredients in a fine-mesh strainer, then sift them in a fine-mesh strainer. If the recipe calls for creaming the vegan butter with the sugar, cream the vegan butter with the sugar. The recipe you are making has been tested and failing to follow a step could mean that the recipe may not come out right. Additionally, if you have to mix a lot of ingredients, do it in separate bowls. Designate one bowl for the dry ingredients and a separate bowl for the wet ingredients. Most recipes will call for adding the wet ingredients to the dry ingredients instead of adding the dry ingredients to the wet ingredients. The former helps you mix the batter more effectively and creates a better texture.

Kitchen Equipment

Most people believe kitchen gadgets are a waste of time and money. While some gadgets, such as egg crackers, are a waste of time, some gadgets are must-haves. For example, having a stand mixer or electric handheld mixer can be lifesaving for creaming butter and sugar for cakes and cookies or making coconut whipped cream. You will also need to purchase cake pans, baking sheets, silicone baking mats, or parchment paper. It would also be useful to invest in a rolling pin, muffin pans, and cookie cutters. Remember, these items are essential and worth the money.

Oven Tips

Make sure your oven is working before you place any food into it. Trust me when I tell you there's nothing worse than making a cake only to realize your oven is not working. To test your oven's temperature, set it to 320 °F (160 °C). After 10 minutes, measure the oven's temperature using a thermometer. This will allow you to determine if your oven runs hot or cool and adjust its temperature if need be. For example, if your oven is too hot at 350 °F (175 °C), you can set your oven to 325°F (163 °C) to prevent your baked goods from burning. This will help you determine where the hot and cold spots in the oven are so you can modify the baking time or temperature. In addition to this, you should always pre-heat your oven. It doesn't matter whether you are making a cake or chocolate chip cookies; pre-heating the oven will ensure they bake evenly.

Ingredients

Vegan baking is a one-of-a-kind baking technique that includes making sweet and savory products. One can choose from a selection of plant-based ingredients providing functionality and great taste with little to no difference in flavor. When choosing vegan baking, substitutes don't need to lack nutrients or taste. Some substitutes give the same fluffiness, softness, and texture!

Most vegan baking ingredients include staples such as flour, sugar, and baking powder, which are essentially the same as non-vegan food. However, there are certain products you should look out for when you are shopping.

Sugar

Most brands of sugars are considered vegan since they are not bleached with bone char. However, you should read the ingredient list or purchase unbleached sugar to err on the side of caution, especially if you do not know where the sugar was sourced from. Most recipes call for caster sugar or superfine sugar, which is ground more finely than table sugar to create a delicate spongy texture in cakes, muffins, or cupcakes. If the recipe calls for liquid sweetener, you can choose between golden syrup, maple syrup, agave nectar, or sugar-free sweeteners like swerve, stevia, monk fruit, or allulose. You can also use corn syrup; however, you should pay attention to where the corn was produced and whether or not it was genetically modified. Recipes may also use fruit sweeteners such as dates instead of traditional sugar.

Vegan Butter and Oils

Fat not only adds color and flavor but it serves as an emulsifier. Margarine is the cheapest type of vegan butter, but there are also vegan butters made from cashews or olive oil. Nevertheless, there is a wide selection of vegan butter found in your local grocery store. If you do not feel comfortable using vegan butter, you can use vegan shortening. However, vegan shortening is best for pastries such as pie crusts or biscuits, not oatmeal cookies. Some recipes replace butter with oil, so you will want to use a neutral-flavored oil like coconut oil, grapeseed oil, or vegetable oil. If you use strong-flavored oils, such as olive oil, it will add a different flavor to your baked goods. Earth Balance makes a great vegan butter product for baking.

Oil makes a suitable vegan substitute when baking and does not allow the batter to stick to the pans or containers. Apart from the substitutes mentioned in the upcoming table, one can also use avocado oil. It is important to note that each oil has different smoking points and heat level tolerance before they ultimately start burning. For example, coconut oil makes a good replacement for vegan butter as it has a low smoking point. On the other hand, oils like avocado oil or sunflower oil have a high smoke point and are good for stir-frying.

Before using these substituents, it is essential to note any allergies, especially when using nut-obtained oils.

Flour And Leavening Agents

Although there was a debate about whether wheat flour is bleached using bone char, this myth has been dispelled. Therefore, all flour, including all-purpose and whole wheat flour, is vegan. There are also flourless recipes in this book that utilizes ingredients such as almond or coconut flour. Nevertheless, there are several different types of flour that will have different effects on how the baked good turns out. Therefore, you should always pay special attention to the leavening agents. The leavening agents used in this baking book are baking powder and baking soda. These leavening agents provide height and give baked goods a light and fluffy texture. Leavening agents are best for cakes, biscuits, muffins, and scones, but they are not ideal for pies and tarts.

Egg Substitutes

Eggs serve several purposes, including adding moisture, structure, and lift to baked goods and binding them together. Eggs are not vegan. Therefore, you must use a substitute. Different egg substitutes serve different purposes. There are vegan egg powders available on the market in which you add water to create a vegan egg. However,

I prefer to use natural egg substitutes such as ground flaxseed meal and water. You can also use plant-based milk such as coconut or almond milk, bananas, applesauce, beans, and chia seeds.

Bananas make an excellent substitute for eggs when cooking cakes, muffins, and brownies. Flaxseed can be mixed with 3 tablespoons of water to create a flax egg. This mixture of flaxseed and water is high in fiber. Chickpea water or Aquafaba is regularly used in baking as an alternative to eggs. These need to be whisked thoroughly before use. Vegan macaroons, mousse, and butter icing all involve the use of this byproduct to create smooth textures.

Milk substitutes

Milk is considered the staple ingredient in baking. There are multiple vegan versions of this dairy product to choose from. Many bakers prefer soy milk because of its high protein content and because it reacts similarly to milk; it's also perfect for producing dairy-free buttermilk. Simply stir a tablespoon of lemon juice, white vinegar, or apple cider vinegar into a cup of sugar-free soy milk and set aside for up to ten minutes.

Honey

Most vegans avoid honey as well as some other sweetening products for ethical reasons and choose plant-obtained sweeteners and syrups instead.

Agave nectar usage can be used to mimic a similar taste to honey, but it is important to be aware that there are some health-related questions attached to it. Maple syrup is another highly used product by bakers with a different taste than honey, but it works very well in baking.

Sorghum is a crop that is heat and drought-tolerant and made into a syrup that is available at most grocery stores. It is just as sweet as honey and can be added in a one-to-one ratio.

Yogurt substitutes

The dairy-free yogurt substitutes used in baking have different textures and tastes depending on the plant they are obtained from. Coconut and oat-obtained yogurt are known to have the creamiest textures, and their use is highly encouraged in the industry.

The use of almond yogurt is also highly encouraged in the baking industry because of its high protein content. It is essential to note that any kind of nut yogurt can cause allergies in some people and should be added with precaution.

Table of substitutes for Vegan baking

Product Name	Substitutes
Dairy Milk	<ul><li>Almond milk</li><li>Macadamia milk</li><li>Soy milk</li><li>Coconut milk</li><li>Oat milk</li><li>Hemp milk</li><li>Quinoa milk</li><li>Pea milk</li><li>Rice milk</li></ul>
Butter	<ul><li>Vegan Butter</li><li>Coconut Oil</li><li>Olive Oil</li><li>Nut Butter</li><li>Mashed Banana</li><li>Mashed Avocado</li><li>Margarine</li><li>Vegetable shortening</li><li>Vegetable oil</li><li>Grapeseed oil</li></ul>
Eggs	<ul><li>Aquafaba (Chickpea Cooking Liquid)</li><li>Ground Flax Seed</li><li>Chia Seeds</li><li>Arrowroot Powder</li><li>Applesauce</li><li>Mashed Banana</li><li>Water, Oil, and Baking Powder</li><li>Carbonated Water</li><li>Beans</li></ul>

Honey or Sweeteners	<ul><li>Agave nectar</li><li>Brown rice syrup</li><li>Coconut nectar</li><li>Maple syrup</li></ul>
Yogurt	<ul><li>Soy yogurt</li><li>Coconut milk yogurt</li><li>Almond milk yogurt</li><li>Cashew-based yogurt</li><li>Pili nut yogurt</li><li>Oat milk yogurt</li><li>Flax milk yogurt</li></ul>
Whipped cream	<ul><li>Whipped Coconut Cream</li></ul>

Now that you've got the basics of vegan baking down, it's time to start baking! Soon you will become a seasoned vegan baker preparing baked goods your friends and family will love.

CHAPTER 1:

COOKIES AND BARS

- Peanut Butter Cookies
- Blackberry Crumble Bars
- Oatmeal Cookies
- Spiced Cookies
- Buckwheat Apple Nut Cookies
- Peanut Butter Bars
- Chocolate Chip Cookies
- Chocolate Pecan Cookies
- Lemon Bars
- Cashew Coconut Lemon Cookies
- Carrot Cookies
- Cherry And Strawberry Thumbprint Cookies
- Pecan Bars
- Almond Crescent Cookies
- Apple Oatmeal Bars

PEANUT BUTTER COOKIES

Peanut butter cookies are a delicious classic treat that's best enjoyed fresh. Best of all, there are little bits of crushed peanuts in every bite, and they are made with natural peanut butter so there are no additives or preservatives in these cookies.

Prep Time: 40 minutes| Cook Time: 15 minutes|
Chill Time: 30 minutes| Total
Time: 1 hour 25 minutes| Servings: 24 cookies

Ingredients

- 1 tablespoon (15 ml) ground flax seed
- 3 tablespoons (45 ml) water
- ½ cup (120 ml) cold vegan butter
- ¾ cup (180 ml) granulated sugar
- ⅓ cup (80 ml) light brown sugar
- 1 teaspoon (5 ml) vanilla extract
- ¾ cup (180 ml) natural peanut butter
- 1 ⅔ cup (395 ml) all-purpose flour
- 1 teaspoon (5 ml) baking soda
- ½ teaspoon (2.5 ml) sea salt
- ⅓ cup (80 ml) crushed peanuts

Instructions

1. Whisk the flaxseed and water in a bowl and allow to sit until it thickens up.
2. Whisk the all-purpose flour, baking soda, and salt in a separate bowl.
3. Place the vegan butter, ½ cup (120 ml) granulated sugar, and brown sugar into a stand mixer outfitted with the paddle attachment and beat it for 3 minutes until it is light and fluffy.
4. Add the flaxseed mixture and vanilla extract and beat for 1 minute.
5. Scrape the sides of the stand mixer's bowl and beat the butter and flaxseed mixture for another minute.
6. Add the peanut butter and beat the peanut butter cookie batter for 1 minute until it is combined.

7. Add the all-purpose flour mixture to the butter flaxseed mixture ingredients and mix just until combined.

8. Fold in the crushed peanuts, then cover the peanut butter cookie batter with plastic wrap and refrigerate the cookie dough for 30 minutes.

9. Turn your oven to 350 °F (175 °C), then place the remaining ¼ cup (60 ml) of granulated sugar into a small bowl.

10. Form the cookie dough into 24 balls, then dredge each ball in the sugar.

11. Place the cookies onto a parchment-lined cookie sheet 1 ½-inches (4 cm) apart, then flatten them with a fork.

12. Bake the cookies for 11-12 minutes until they are slightly golden.

13. Let the peanut butter cookies cool on the pan for 5 minutes, then place them onto a wire rack.

14. Serve and enjoy!

BLACKBERRY CRUMBLE BARS

These blackberries crumble bars are buttery and crumbly. The blackberry filling is sweet yet tangy and has a hint of spice from cardamom and nutmeg.

Prep Time: 40 minutes| Cook Time: 15 minutes|
Total Time: 55 minutes| Servings: 8 bars

Ingredients

For the crust and topping:

- 3 cups (705 ml) all-purpose flour
- 1 ½ cups (355 ml) granulated sugar
- zest of 1 large lemon
- ½ cup (120 ml) unsalted vegan butter, chilled, cut into cubes
- 3 tablespoons (45 ml) flax meal
- 9 tablespoons water (135 ml)

For the blackberry filling:

- 4 cups (940 ml) blackberries, halved
- juice of 1 lemon
- ⅛ teaspoon (.6 ml) nutmeg
- ⅛ teaspoon (.6 ml) ground cardamom
- 1 tablespoon (15 ml) cornstarch
- ¾ cup (180ml) granulated sugar

Instructions

1. Whisk the flax meal with the water and set aside.
2. Turn your oven to 350 °F (175 °C), then line a 9 by 13 baking pan with parchment paper.
3. Whisk the all-purpose flour, sugar, and lemon zest in a bowl, then add the cold butter and break the butter into small pea-sized pieces with your fingertips.
4. Stir in the flax meal mixture until a crumbly dough forms.
5. Press half of the crumbly dough mixture into the prepared baking pan and set it aside.

6. For the blackberry filling, mix the blackberries, lemon juice, nutmeg, cardamom, cornstarch, and sugar in another bowl.
7. Pour the blackberry filling mixture into the crust, then add the remaining dough over the filling.
8. Bake for 35-40 minutes until they are golden brown.
9. Let the blackberry crumble bars cool completely before cutting them into 8 bars.
10. Serve and enjoy!

OATMEAL COOKIES

Oatmeal cookies are a delicious classic. But sometimes, classics can get boring. Luckily, we added cinnamon and cardamom to add a warm, delicious flavor to the oatmeal cookies. The chocolate chips add a sweet flavor and texture to the oatmeal cookies.

Prep Time: 10 minutesl Cook Time: 16 minutesl
Total Time: 26 minutesl Servings: 12 cookies

Ingredients

- ½ cup (120 ml) unsalted vegan butter, softened
- ½ cup (120 ml) dark brown sugar
- ½ cup (120 ml) granulated sugar
- 1 ½ cups (355 ml) all-purpose flour
- 1 ½ cups (355 ml) old fashioned rolled oats
- 1 teaspoon (5 ml) baking powder
- 1 teaspoon (5 ml) baking soda
- 1 teaspoon (5 ml) cinnamon
- ½ teaspoon (2.5 ml) cardamom
- ¼ teaspoon (1 ml) salt
- ⅓ cup (80 ml) coconut milk
- ⅓ cup (80 ml) chocolate chips

Instructions

1. Line a cookie sheet with parchment paper.
2. Whisk the oats, all-purpose flour, baking powder, baking soda, cinnamon, cardamom, and salt in a bowl and set it aside.
3. Beat the vegan butter in a stand mixer fitted with the paddle attachment for 30 seconds.
4. Next, add the dark brown sugar and granulated sugar to the butter and beat it for 2 minutes until light and fluffy.
5. Add the oat and all-purpose flour mixture and beat until a crumbly mixture forms.
6. Add the coconut milk and beat it for 1 minute until a dough forms, then fold in the chocolate chips.

7. Scoop the oatmeal cookies using a 2 tablespoon (30 ml) cookie scoop and place them onto the prepared cookie sheet 2-inches (5 cm) apart.

8. Loosely cover the cookies with plastic wrap and place them in the fridge for 20 minutes.

9. Set the oven to 350 °F (175 °C).

10. Bake the cookies for 14-16 minutes until they are slightly golden.

11. Let the chocolate chip oatmeal cookies cool on the pan, then transfer them to a wire rack to cool completely.

12. Serve and enjoy!

SPICED COOKIES

Warm cookies filled with spices? Yes, please! These spiced cookies are filled with warm fall flavors. Just one bite and these spiced cookies will be your new favorite cookie.

Prep Time: 15 minutesl Cook Time: 12 minutesl
Chill Time: 1 hourl Total Time: 1 hour 27 minutesl
Servings: 16

Ingredients

- 1 tablespoon (15 ml) ground flaxseed meal
- 3 tablespoons (45 ml) water
- 1 ¼ (295 ml) cups all-purpose flour
- 1 teaspoon (5 ml) ground ginger
- 1 ½ teaspoons (7.5 ml) ground cinnamon
- ½ teaspoon (2.5 ml) ground cardamom
- ½ teaspoon (2.5 ml) ground cloves
- ½ teaspoon (2.5 ml) ground star anise
- 1 teaspoon (5 ml) baking soda
- ¼ teaspoon (1 ml) salt

- 6 tablespoons (90 ml) vegan butter, softened
- ¾ cup (180 ml) dark brown sugar
- 6 tablespoons (90 ml) natural almond butter
- 1 ½ teaspoons (7.5 ml) vanilla extract
- 2 tablespoons (30 ml) powdered sugar

Instructions

1. Whisk the flaxseed meal and water in a bowl and let it sit for 5-10 minutes.
2. Whisk the all-purpose flour, 1 teaspoon ground ginger, cinnamon, cardamom, cloves, star anise, baking soda, and salt in a bowl.
3. Beat the butter, brown sugar, almond butter, and vanilla extract in a stand mixer fitted with the paddle attachment on medium for 30 seconds to 1 minute.
4. Add the flaxseed water mixture and mix on low until combined.
5. Add the spiced all-purpose flour mixture and mix until incorporated.

6. Cover the cookie dough and chill it in the fridge for 1 hour.
7. Set the oven to 350 °F (175 °C) and line a cookie sheet with parchment paper.
8. Roll the cookie dough into 6 balls, then place them onto the prepared pan 2-inches (5 cm) apart.
9. Gently press the cookies down with the palm of your hand.
10. Bake the cookies for 10-12 minutes until golden around the edges.
11. Let them cool on the pan for 5 minutes, then place them on a wire rack to cool.
12. Lightly dust the spiced cookies with powdered sugar.
13. Serve and enjoy!

BUCKWHEAT APPLE NUT COOKIES

These buckwheat apple nut cookies are super delicious and healthy. They are made with toasted hazelnuts and spices such as cinnamon and nutmeg. Best of all, these buckwheat apple nut cookies are gluten-free.

Prep Time: 15 minutes| Cook Time: 10 minutes|
Total Time: 25 minutes| Servings: 24 cookies

Ingredients

- ½ cup (120 ml) vegan butter, melted
- ¼ cup (60 ml) mashed bananas
- ¾ cup (180 ml) date paste
- 1 teaspoon (5 ml) pure vanilla extract
- ¼ cup (60 ml) buckwheat flour
- 1 ¼ cup (295 ml) almond flour
- 1 cup (235 ml) instant oats
- ½ teaspoon (2.5 ml) cinnamon
- ¼ teaspoon (1 ml) nutmeg
- ¼ teaspoon (1 ml) cloves
- ¼ teaspoon (1 ml) sea salt

- ½ teaspoon (2.5 ml) baking soda
- 1 cup (235 ml) peeled, diced apples
- ⅓ cup (80 ml) crushed toasted hazelnuts

Instructions

1. Turn the oven to 350 °F (175 °C).
2. Whisk the butter, mashed bananas, date paste, and vanilla extract in a large bowl.
3. Add the buckwheat flour, almond flour, oats, cinnamon, nutmeg, cloves, sea salt, and baking soda in another bowl.
4. Add the buckwheat flour oat mixture to the butter banana mixture and stir to combine.
5. Fold in the diced apples and hazelnuts and mix until combined.
6. Scoop the cookies using a 2-3 tablespoon (30 - 45 ml) cookie scoop, then roll them into balls.
7. Place the cookies onto a cookie sheet lined with parchment paper.

8. Bake the buckwheat apple nut cookies for 10-12 minutes until slightly golden.
9. Let the pan cool on the pan for 5 minutes, then place them onto a wire rack to cool completely.
10. Serve and enjoy!

PEANUT BUTTER BARS

These peanut butter bars are rich, decadent, and delicious. Best of all, these they are no-bake and gluten-free. Coated with a chocolate topping, these bars are a tasty snack or dessert.

Prep Time: 10 minutes| Cook Time: 5 minutes|
Total Time: 15 minutes| Servings: 8 bars

Ingredients

For the peanut butter bars:

- 1 cup (235 ml) natural peanut butter
- ¼ cup (60 ml) maple syrup
- 1 teaspoon (5 ml) vanilla extract
- ¼ teaspoon (1 ml) fine sea salt
- ½ cup (120 ml) vegan protein powder
- ½ cup (120 ml) almond flour

For the topping:

- 1 cup (235 ml) dark chocolate chips
- ½ cup (120 ml) natural peanut butter
- 2 tablespoons (30 ml) powdered sugar

Instructions

1. Line an 8 by 8-inch baking pan with parchment paper and set it aside.
2. To make the base, mix the peanut butter, maple syrup, vanilla extract, sea salt, protein powder, and almond flour in a bowl until combined.
3. Press the peanut butter base into the prepared baking dish.
4. To make the topping, add the peanut butter and chocolate chips into a microwave-safe bowl.
5. Heat the peanut butter chocolate mixture in 30-second intervals, stirring after each interval until it is melted.
6. Pour the melted mixture over the base and spread it into an even layer.
7. Freeze the bars for 1 hour until set.
8. Slice the peanut butter bars into 8 bars and dust them with the powdered sugar.
9. Serve and enjoy!

CHOCOLATE CHIP COOKIES

Chocolate chip cookies are a decadent classic. While there is nothing wrong with traditional chocolate chip cookies, I decided to add a pinch of instant coffee to enhance the cookie's flavor even more.

Prep Time: 10 minutes| Cook Time: 12 minutes|
Chill Time: 1 hour| Total Time: 1 hour 22 minutes|
Servings: 24

Ingredients

- 1 tablespoon (15 ml) ground flaxseed
- 3 tablespoons (45 ml) water
- 1 ¼ cups (295 ml) all-purpose flour
- 1 teaspoon (5 ml) baking soda
- 1 teaspoon (5 ml) instant coffee
- ¼ teaspoon (1 ml) fine salt
- ½ cup (120 ml) unsalted vegan butter, softened
- ½ cup (120 ml) packed light brown sugar

- ⅓ cup (80 ml) granulated sugar
- 1 teaspoon (5 ml) vanilla extract
- 1 ½ cups (355 ml) semisweet chocolate chips

Instructions

1. Whisk the flaxseed and water in a bowl and let it sit for 5-10 minutes.
2. Whisk all-purpose flour, baking soda, instant coffee, and salt in a bowl.
3. Place the softened butter, brown sugar, and granulated sugar into a stand mixer outfitted with the paddle attachment and beat for 2 minutes until it is fluffy.
4. Add the flaxseed mixture and vanilla extract and mix on low just until it is combined.
5. Add the flour coffee mixture in two batches and beat on low until combined.
6. Next, stir the chocolate chips into the dough, then cover the chocolate chip cookie dough.
7. Chill the chocolate chip cookie dough in the fridge for 1 hour.
8. Set the oven to 350 °F (175 °C), then line a baking sheet with parchment paper.

9. Using a 2-3 tablespoon cookie scoop, scoop the chocolate chip cookies onto the prepared pan, leaving 2-inches of space between each cookie.
10. Place the cookies into the oven and bake them for 10-12 minutes until the edges of the cookies are slightly golden.
11. Let the chocolate chip cookies cool on the baking sheet for 5 minutes, then place them on a cooling rack to cool.
12. Serve and enjoy!

CHOCOLATE PECAN COOKIES

Chocolate and pecans are a stellar combination. These chocolate pecan cookies are no different. They are soft yet chewy, with sweet, buttery, nutty pecans in every bite.

Prep Time: 20 minutesl Cook Time: 12 minsl Total Time: 32 minutesl Servings: 12 cookies

Ingredients

- 1 tablespoon (15 ml) ground flaxseed
- 3 tablespoons (45 ml) water
- ¾ cup (180 ml) all-purpose flour
- ⅓ cup (80 ml) Dutch-processed cocoa powder
- 2 tablespoons (30 ml) cornstarch
- 1 teaspoon (5 ml) coffee
- 1 teaspoon (5 ml) baking powder
- ½ tsp (2.5 ml) baking soda
- ⅛ teaspoon (.6 ml) salt
- 10 tablespoons (150 ml) unsalted vegan butter, softened

- ⅓ cup (80 ml) brown sugar packed
- ⅓ cup (80 ml) granulated sugar
- 1 teaspoon (5 ml) vanilla extract
- ½ cup (120 ml) pecans, chopped

Instructions

1. Turn the oven to 350 °F (175 °C) and line two baking sheets with parchment paper.
2. Whisk the flaxseed meal and water in a bowl and let it sit for 5-10 minutes.
3. Whisk the all-purpose flour, cocoa powder, cornstarch, coffee, baking powder, baking soda, and salt in a bowl until well combined.
4. Place the softened butter, brown sugar, and granulated sugar into a stand mixer outfitted with the paddle attachment and beat for 2 minutes until fluffy.
5. Add the flaxseed mixture and vanilla extract and beat until combined.
6. Add the all-purpose flour cocoa powder mixture, mix just until a dough forms, then fold in the pecans.

7. Divide the cookie dough into 12 uniform balls and place them on the prepared cookie sheets 2-inches (5 cm) apart.
8. Press the cookies with your hand to flatten them slightly and bake for 11-12 minutes.
9. Let the chocolate pecan cookies cool on the pan for 10 minutes, then place them on a cooling rack to cool.
10. Serve and enjoy!

LEMON BARS

These lemon bars are incredibly delicious. Not only is there lemon juice and zest in the filling, but there is also lemon zest in the buttery shortbread crust. Furthermore, coconut cream makes the lemon filling super creamy and delicious!

Prep Time: 15 minutesl Cook Time: 35 minutesl
Chilling Time: 2 hoursl
Total Time: 2 hours 50 minutesl Servings: 16 bars

Ingredients

For the shortbread crust:

- ¼ cup (60 ml) granulated sugar
- 1 cup (235 ml) all-purpose flour
- ¼ teaspoon (1 ml) salt
- 1 teaspoon (5 ml) lemon zest
- ½ cup (120 ml) vegan butter, melted

For the lemon filling:

- ¾ cup (180 ml) fresh lemon juice
- 2 teaspoons (10 ml) lemon zest
- 1 ¼ cups (295 ml) granulated sugar
- ¼ cup (60 ml) agave nectar
- 1 cup (235 ml) full-fat coconut milk
- ¼ cup (60 ml) coconut cream
- 6 tablespoons (90 ml) arrowroot powder
- 1 teaspoon (5 ml) yellow food coloring

For serving:

- 3 tablespoons (45 ml) powdered sugar
- candied lemon peel, cut into small strips

Instructions

1. Turn your oven to 350 °F (175 °C), then line a 9 by 13 baking pan with parchment paper.

2. To make the shortbread crust, whisk the all-purpose flour, sugar, salt, and lemon zest in a bowl.

3. Add the melted vegan butter to the flour mixture and mix until a dough forms.

4. Press the shortbread crust into the prepared pan in an even layer using your hands.

5. Bake the crust for 16-18 minutes until the edges are lightly browned, then set it aside.

6. To make the lemon filling, whisk the lemon juice, lemon zest, granulated sugar, coconut milk, coconut cream, arrowroot powder, and yellow food coloring well in a saucepan.

7. Place the lemon filling over medium-high heat and cook it for 5-10 minutes, constantly stirring until the filling thickens up.

8. Add the lemon filling to the shortbread crust and spread it into an even layer.

9. Bake the lemon bars for 15 minutes, then remove them from the oven and let cool for 30 minutes on a wire rack.

10. Chill the bars in the fridge for 2 hours or overnight, until set.

11. Remove the bars from the pan. Place the powdered sugar into a fine-mesh sieve and dust the bars with powdered sugar.

12. Next, slice the lemon bars into 16 squares and garnish each bar with lemon peel.

13. Serve and enjoy!

CASHEW COCONUT LEMON COOKIES

The rich nutty flavor of cashews meets the sweet flavor of coconut and the tart flavor of lemon; what a combination! These cashew coconut lemon cookies even contain a pinch of ginger and cardamom for a burst of warm flavor.

Prep Time: 10 minutes| Cook Time: 12 minutes|
Total Time: 22 minutes| Servings: 10-12 cookies

Ingredients:

- 1 tablespoon (15 ml) ground flaxseed meal
- 3 tablespoons (45 ml) water
- 1 ½ cups (355 ml) raw cashews
- ¼ cup (60 ml) coconut flour
- ¼ teaspoon (1 ml) ground ginger
- ⅛ teaspoon (.6 ml) cardamom
- ¼ cup (60 ml) melted coconut oil
- 3 tablespoons (45 ml) pure maple syrup
- ¼ teaspoon (1 ml) sea salt
- ½ teaspoon (2.5 ml) baking soda

- 1 teaspoon (5 ml) lemon extract
- zest of 1 lemon
- ¼ cup (60 ml) unsweetened shredded coconut

Instructions

1. Combine the ground flaxseed meal and water in a small bowl and set it aside for 5 minutes until it thickens.
2. Turn your oven to 350 °F (175 °C), then line 2 cookie sheets with parchment paper.
3. Place 1 cup (235 ml) of cashews into a food processor and process them into fine crumbs.
4. Add the coconut flour, ginger, and cardamom, and pulse until the cashew mixture resembles is a flour-like powder.
5. Add the coconut oil, maple syrup, flaxseed mixture, lemon extract, lemon zest, salt, baking soda, and shredded coconut and pulse until a ball forms.

6. With a tablespoon (15 ml) cookie scoop, scoop the cookie dough into balls and place them onto the prepared cookie sheets.
7. Flatten the cookies slightly and press 1 cashew into the middle of each cookie.
8. Bake the cookies for 11-12 minutes until the edges of the cookies start to turn golden brown.
9. Let the cashew coconut lemon cookies cool on the pan for 5 minutes, then place them on a wire rack to cool completely.
10. Serve and enjoy!

CARROT COOKIES

Why wait for an event, holiday, or special occasion to make an entire carrot cake when you can easily make carrot cookies. You will get the same great flavor of carrot cake in cookie form. Best of all, you can make these cookies anytime you are in the mood for carrot cake.

Prep Time: 10 minutesl Cook Time: 10 minutesl
Total Time: 20 minutesl Serves: 12 cookies

Ingredients

- 1 cup (235 ml) old fashioned rolled oats
- ¾ cup (180 ml) all-purpose flour
- 1 ½ teaspoons (7.5 ml) baking powder
- 1 teaspoon (5 ml) cinnamon
- ¼ teaspoon (1 ml) nutmeg
- ¼ teaspoon (1 ml) cloves
- 2 tablespoons (30 ml) melted vegan butter
- ½ cup (120 ml) coconut milk
- ½ cup (120 ml) mashed bananas
- 1 teaspoon (5 ml) vanilla extract
- 1 cup (235 ml) brown sugar
- 1 cup (235 ml) carrot finely grated

Instructions

1. Turn your oven to 325 °F (163 °C), then line 2 cookie sheets with parchment paper.
2. Whisk the oats, all-purpose flour, baking powder, cinnamon, nutmeg, and cloves in a bowl.
3. Whisk the coconut milk, mashed bananas, vanilla extract, melted butter, and brown sugar in another bowl.
4. In two portions, stir the oat flour mixture into the wet ingredients just until combined.
5. Fold in the shredded carrots.
6. With a tablespoon cookie scoop, scoop the cookie dough into balls and place them onto the prepared cookie sheets.
7. Bake the cookies for 8-10 minutes until lightly browned around the edges.

8. Let the carrot cookies cool on the cookie sheet for 5 minutes, then place them onto a wire rack to cool completely.

9. Serve and enjoy!

CHERRY AND STRAWBERRY THUMBPRINT COOKIES

Thumbprint cookies are buttery delights that are stuffed with jam or preserves. Instead of using a single preserve, these cookies are filled with cherry and strawberry preserves. With two different flavors of thumbprint cookies, there's something for everyone in this batch of cookies.

Prep Time: 15 minutesl Cook Time: 15 minutesl
Total Time: 30 minutesl Serves: 26 cookies

Ingredients

For the thumbprint cookies:

- 2 ½ cups (590 ml) all-purpose flour
- ¾ cup (180 ml) powdered sugar
- 1 ¼ cups (295 ml) vegan butter, softened
- 1 teaspoon (5 ml) vanilla extract
- ¼ cup (60 ml) strawberry preserves
- ¼ cup (60 ml) cherry preserves

For the vanilla glaze:

- 1 cup (235 ml) powdered sugar
- 1 teaspoon (5 ml) vanilla bean paste
- 2-3 teaspoons (10-15 ml) water

Instructions

1. Turn your oven to 325 °F (163 °C), then line 2 cookie sheets with parchment paper.
2. Place the all-purpose and powdered sugar into a stand mixer outfitted with the paddle attachment. Mix for 30 seconds to combine.
3. Add the softened butter to the flour powdered sugar mixture along with the vanilla extract and mix until a crumbly mixture forms. The cookie dough should be crumbly, but it should hold together when it is smushed.
4. Form the cookie dough into 1-inch balls that are about a tablespoon and place them onto the prepared baking sheets.
5. Make a small impression in each cookie dough ball using your thumb.

6. Fill each impression with cherry or strawberry preserves.
7. Place the cookies into the freezer for 10 minutes.
8. Bake the cookies for 15-16 minutes until they are lightly golden around the edges.
9. Let the thumbprint cookies cool on the cookie sheet for 5 minutes, then place them onto a wire rack to cool completely.
10. To make the vanilla glaze, whisk the sugar, vanilla bean paste, and water in a bowl until it is smooth and thick.
11. Place the vanilla glaze into a small piping bag and cut a small hole in the bag. Drizzle the vanilla glaze over the cookies.
12. Serve and enjoy!

PECAN BARS

Caramel filling studded with chopped pecans and a buttery shortbread crust? Yes, please! These pecan bars are absolutely delicious. The shortbread crust contains cinnamon and orange zest to cut through the buttery richness of the dough, while the filling is made with sweet maple syrup and brown sugar.

Prep Time: 15 minutes| Cook Time: 40 minutes|
Total Time: 55 minutes| Serves: 16 bars

Ingredients

For the shortbread crust:

- 2 cups (470 ml) all-purpose flour
- ½ cup (120 ml) granulated white sugar
- ¼ teaspoon (1 ml) salt
- 1 teaspoon (5 ml) orange zest
- ⅛ teaspoon (.6 ml) cinnamon
- ¾ cup (180 ml) cold vegan butter, cut into cubes

For the pecan topping:

- 1 cup (235 ml) brown sugar
- ¾ cup (180 ml) maple syrup
- 3 tablespoons (45 ml) almond milk
- 3 tablespoons (45 ml) melted vegan butter
- 3 tablespoons (45 ml) arrowroot powder
- 1 teaspoon (5 ml) vanilla bean paste
- 2 cups (470 ml) coarsely chopped pecans

Instructions

1. Turn your oven to 350 °F (175 °C), then line a 9 by 13 baking pan with parchment paper.
2. To make the shortbread crust, whisk the all-purpose flour, sugar, salt, orange zest, and cinnamon in a bowl.

3. Add the vegan butter to the bowl, and using a pastry cutter or two knives, cut it into the all-purpose flour mixture until it looks like fine crumbs.

4. Place the shortbread crust into the prepared pan and press it in an even layer.

5. Bake the crust for 10 minutes, then set it aside to cool slightly.

6. To make the pecan topping, whisk the brown sugar, maple syrup, almond milk, vegan butter, vanilla bean paste, and arrowroot powder in a large bowl until it is smooth.

7. Fold in the chopped pecans. Add the pecan toppings to the shortbread crust and spread it into an even layer.

8. Bake the pecan shortbread for 25-30 minutes until the pecan topping bubbles.

9. Remove the bars from the oven and let them cool on a wire rack for 30 minutes.

10. Place the bars into the fridge for at least 2-3 hours to set.

11. Remove the pecan bars from the pan and cut them into 16 bars.

12. Serve and enjoy!

ALMOND CRESCENT COOKIES

Crescent cookies or Viennese crescents are Austrian cookies that are usually given as a Christmas gift. These almond crescent cookies are baked until lightly golden, then rolled in powdered sugar to create the best gluten-free, buttery, and delicious cookies.

Prep Time: 10 minutes| Cook Time: 15 minutes|
Total Time: 25 minutes| Serves: 20 cookies

Ingredients

- ½ cup (120 ml) vegan butter softened
- ⅓ cup (80 ml) granulated white sugar
- 1 tablespoon (15 ml) pure almond extract
- ¾ cup (180 ml) finely ground almond flour
- ¾ cup (180 ml) gluten-free all-purpose flour
- ¼ teaspoon (1 ml) sea salt
- ½ cup (120 ml) powdered sugar

Instructions

1. Turn your oven to 325 °F (163 °C), then line 2 cookie sheets with parchment paper.
2. Place the vegan butter, granulated sugar, and almond extract into a stand mixer outfitted with the paddle attachment and mix for 1-2 seconds until fluffy.
3. Whisk the almond flour, gluten-free all-purpose flour, and salt in a bowl.
4. Add the gluten-free flour mixture to the butter-sugar mixture and mix to combine.
5. Roll 1 tablespoon (15 ml) of the crescent cookie dough into a log, then form it into a crescent shape.
6. Place the cookie onto the prepared cookie sheet and continue rolling and shaping the cookie dough into crescents.
7. Bake the cookies for 15 minutes until golden brown.

8. Let the cookies cool on the cookie sheet for 5 minutes, then place them onto a wire rack to cool slightly.

9. Place the powdered sugar into a shallow bowl. While the crescent cookies are still warm, roll them in the powdered sugar.

10. Serve and enjoy!

APPLE OATMEAL BARS

These apple oatmeal bars are healthy, gluten-free, and sugar-free. Baked until they are golden brown, these apple oatmeal bars are so delicious that one bar of these guilt-free pleasures is simply not enough.

Prep Time: 10 minutesl Cook Time: 40 minutesl
Total Time: 50 minutesl Serves: 9 bars

Ingredients

- 1 tablespoon (15 ml) ground flaxseed meal
- 3 tablespoons (45 ml) water
- 1 cup (235 ml) oat flour
- 1 ½ (355 ml) cups certified gluten-free old-fashioned oats
- 1 ½ (7.5 ml) teaspoons cinnamon
- ¼ teaspoon (1 ml) ground allspice
- ½ teaspoon (2.5 ml) baking powder
- ¼ teaspoon (1 ml) salt
- 1 cup (235 ml) unsweetened almond milk
- 6 tablespoons (90 ml) sugar-free applesauce
- 6 tablespoons (90 ml) pure maple syrup
- ¼ cup (60 ml) vegan butter, melted
- 1 teaspoon (5 ml) vanilla bean paste
- 1 Granny Smith apple, peeled, grated

Instructions

1. Turn your oven to 350 °F (175 °C), then coat an 8 by 8 baking pan with non-stick cooking spray.
2. Mix the ground flaxseed meal and water in a bowl and set it aside for 5 minutes.
3. Whisk the oat flour, oats, cinnamon, allspice, baking powder, and salt in a bowl.
4. In another bowl, whisk the almond milk, applesauce, maple syrup, melted vegan butter, vanilla bean paste, and flaxseed mixture until combined.
5. Stir the oat flour mixture into the wet ingredients.

6. Fold in the apples, then pour the batter into the prepared pan.

7. Bake the bars for 35-40 minutes until the center is set and the edges are golden brown.

8. Allow the apple bars to cool completely before slicing them into 9 bars.

9. Serve and enjoy!

CHAPTER 2:

BREADS, BISCUITS, SCONES AND ROLLS

- Flaky Biscuits
- Black Currant Scones
- Soda Bread
- Banana Carrot Bread
- Blueberry Pumpkin Bread

- Cast-Iron Zucchini Bread
- Lemon Poppy Seed Scones
- Coconut Oat Bread
- Maple Cornbread
- Spiced Orange Cinnamon Rolls

FLAKY BISCUITS

Biscuits are a staple breakfast and brunch food. Whether you add jam to them or make vegan biscuits and gravy, you need to have a good biscuit recipe in your arsenal. The trick to flaky biscuits is using cold ingredients and being gentle with the dough.

Prep Time: 15 minutes| Cook Time: 17 minutes|
Total Time: 32 minutes| Serves: 8 biscuits

Ingredients

- ¾ cup (180 ml) coconut milk
- 1 tablespoon (15 ml) fresh lemon juice
- 1 ½ cups (355 ml) all-purpose flour
- ¼ teaspoon (1 ml) salt
- 1 tablespoon (15 ml) granulated white sugar
- 2 teaspoons (30 ml) baking powder
- 6 tablespoons (90 ml) vegan butter cut into ½-inch pieces
- 2 tablespoons (30 ml) melted vegan butter

Instructions

1. Turn your oven to 400 °F (205 °C), then line a baking sheet with parchment paper.
2. Whisk coconut milk and lemon juice in a small bowl and set it aside for 2 minutes.
3. Whisk the all-purpose flour, salt, sugar, and baking powder in a separate bowl.
4. Add the vegan butter to the bowl and, using a pastry cutter or two knives, cut it into the all-purpose flour mixture until it looks like fine crumbs.
5. Add the coconut milk lemon mixture and stir carefully just until the dough comes together.
6. Place the dough onto a floured surface and knead it lightly a few times until it is not overly sticky.
7. Flatten the dough until it is 1-inch (2.5 cm) in thickness. Gently fold the dough over onto itself and pat it out until it is 1-inch (2.5 cm) in thickness. Fold and flatten the dough two more times.

8. Flatten the biscuit dough until it is ¾-inch in thickness and cut the biscuits out using a circle cookie cutter that has been dipped in flour.
9. Place the biscuits onto a baking sheet and place them in the freezer for 30 minutes.
10. Brush the biscuits with melted vegan butter.
11. Bake them for 15-17 minutes until they are golden brown.
12. Let the biscuits cool for 5 minutes.
13. Serve and enjoy!

BLACK CURRANT SCONES

Black currants have a tart flavor that pairs perfectly with the lightly sweet flavor of the scones. These scones are flavored with vanilla and baked until golden brown. Serve them with strawberry jam for best results.

Prep Time: 15 minutes| Cook Time: 12 minutes|
Total Time: 27 minutes| Serves: 8 scones

Ingredients

- 2 cups (470 ml) all-purpose flour
- 1 tablespoon (15 ml) baking powder
- ¼ cup (60 ml) granulated white sugar
- ¼ teaspoon (1 ml) salt
- ⅛ teaspoon (.6 ml) cinnamon
- 4 tablespoons (60 ml) room temperature coconut oil, cut into small pieces
- ½ cup (120 ml) black currants
- 1 teaspoon (5 ml) vanilla extract
- ⅔ cups (160 ml) coconut milk
- 2 tablespoons (30 ml) melted vegan butter
- 2 tablespoons (30 ml) sanding sugar

Instructions

1. Place the all-purpose flour and baking powder into a fine-mesh strainer and sift it into a bowl.
2. Whisk in the sugar, salt, and cinnamon.
3. Add the coconut oil to the flour, and using a pastry cutter or two knives, cut it into the all-purpose flour mixture until it looks like fine crumbs.
4. Fold in the black currants.
5. Fold in the vanilla extract and coconut milk and mix it using a wooden spoon until the dough comes together.
6. Place the dough onto a lightly floured surface and knead it lightly.
7. Place the dough onto a sheet of parchment paper and shape it into a disc.

8. Using the parchment paper, place scone dough onto a baking sheet and chill it in the fridge for 15 minutes.

9. Turn your oven to 425 °F (218 °C) and line a baking sheet with parchment paper.

10. Remove the scone dough from the fridge and cut it into 8 triangular scones using a sharp knife.

11. Place the scones onto the prepared baking sheet and brush them with melted vegan butter. Sprinkle the sanding sugar over the scones.

12. Bake for 12 minutes.

13. Allow the black currant scones to cool for a few minutes.

14. Serve and enjoy!

SODA BREAD

Even though soda bread is credited to the Irish, Native Americans actually invented soda bread. Native Americans were the first to use pearl ash, an organic form of soda, to leaven bread without yeast. The Irish discovered it and successfully replicated it, giving us the delicious soda bread we know and love today.

Prep Time: 10 minutes| Cook Time: 50 minutes|
Total Time: 1 hour| Serves: 10 slices

Ingredients

- 4 cups (940 ml) all-purpose flour
- 1 tablespoon (15 ml) granulated white sugar
- 1 teaspoon (5 ml) fine sea salt
- 1 ¾ (9 ml) teaspoons baking soda
- ⅓ cup (80 ml) raisins or black currants
- 1 cup (235 ml) unsweetened oat milk
- ½ cup (120 ml) unsweetened cashew yogurt

- 4 tablespoons (60 ml) melted vegan butter
- 1 tablespoon (15 ml) apple cider vinegar

Instructions

1. Turn your oven to 400 °F (205 °C).
2. Whisk the all-purpose flour, sugar, salt, baking soda, and raisins or black currants in a bowl.
3. Whisk the oat milk, cashew yogurt, melted butter, and apple cider vinegar in another bowl until combined.
4. Add the cashew yogurt mixture to the all-purpose flour mixture and mix until a shaggy dough forms. If the soda bread dough is too dry, add 1-2 tablespoons (15 – 30 ml) of oat milk and mix until the dough sticks together.

5. Place the dough onto a floured surface. Dust your hands with flour and knead the dough into a ball. If the soda bread dough is super sticky, add a little more flour.

6. Shape the dough into a dish that is 7-inches in diameter and 2-inches high.

7. Place the soda bread onto a parchment-lined baking sheet. Run a sharp knife under running water and cut a cross about 3/4-inch (2 cm) deep into the soda bread.

8. Bake the bread for 50 minutes until it is firm and golden brown. It should sound hollow when you tap the bottom of the bread.

9. Place the soda bread onto a wire rack and let it cool for at least 30 minutes before slicing.

10. Serve and enjoy!

BANANA CARROT BREAD

Who needs regular banana bread when you can spice it up. Simply add carrots, cinnamon, nutmeg, and walnuts, and you've got a delicious banana carrot bread. Best of all, it is gluten-free.

Prep Time: 15 minutes| Cook Time: 55 minutes|
Total Time: 1 hour 10 minutes| Serves: 10 slices

Ingredients

- ¼ cup (60 ml) coconut flour
- 1 ¼ (295 ml) cups oat flour
- ⅓ cup (80 ml) old fashioned oats
- 2 teaspoons (10 ml) cinnamon
- ½ teaspoon (2.5 ml) nutmeg
- 2 teaspoons (10 ml) baking powder
- ½ teaspoon (2.5 ml) baking soda
- ¼ teaspoon (1 ml) salt
- ⅓ cup (80 ml) granulated white sugar
- ½ cup (120 ml) unsweetened oat milk
- ¼ cup (60 ml) melted vegan butter
- 1 teaspoon (5 ml) vanilla extract

- 3 medium bananas, mashed
- 3 carrots, grated
- ¾ cup (180 ml) chopped walnuts, optional

Instructions

1. Turn your oven to 350 °F (175 °C), then spray a 9 by 5-inch loaf pan with non-stick spray.
2. Whisk the coconut flour, oat flour, oats, cinnamon, nutmeg, baking powder, baking soda, and salt in a large bowl.
3. Whisk the sugar, oat milk, melted butter, vanilla extract, and mashed bananas in a separate bowl.
4. Add the coconut oat flour mixture to the wet ingredients and mix until combined.
5. Fold in the shredded carrots and chopped walnuts, then pour the banana carrot bread into the prepared loaf pan.

6. Bake the bread for 20 minutes, then rotate the pan halfway and bake it for 30-35 minutes.
7. Let the carrot banana bread cool in the pan for 10 minutes, then place it onto a wire rack to cool completely.
8. Serve and enjoy!

BLUEBERRY PUMPKIN BREAD

Pumpkin bread gets jazzed up with fresh sweet blueberries. This blueberry pumpkin bread is flavored by cinnamon, and the blueberries add a burst of purple color to an otherwise plain brown-colored bread.

Prep Time: 10 minutesl Cook Time: 45 minutesl
Total Time: 55 minutes: Serves: 12 slices

Ingredients

- 1 cup (235 ml) pumpkin puree
- 1 cup (235 ml) dark brown sugar, firmly packed
- ½ cup (120 ml) vegetable oil
- 3 tablespoons (45 ml) agave nectar
- 3 tablespoons (45 ml) water
- 1 ¾ cups (415 ml) all-purpose flour
- 1 teaspoon (5 ml) baking soda
- 1 teaspoon (5 ml) baking powder
- ½ teaspoon (2.5 ml) salt

- 1 teaspoon (5 ml) cinnamon
- 1 cup (235 ml) fresh blueberries

Instructions

1. Turn your oven to 350 °F (175 °C), then spray a 9 by 5-inch loaf pan with non-stick spray.
2. Whisk the pumpkin puree, brown sugar, agave nectar, vegetable oil, and water in a bowl until combined.
3. Whisk the all-purpose flour, baking powder and baking soda, salt, and cinnamon, in a separate bowl until combined.
4. Add the all-purpose flour dry mixture to the wet ingredients and mix until combined.
5. Fold in the blueberries, then pour the batter into the prepared pan.
6. Bake the bread for 45-55 minutes until a skewer comes out clean.

7. Let the blueberry pumpkin bread cool in the pan for 15 minutes, then remove from the pan and place onto a wire rack to cool completely.

8. Serve and enjoy!

CAST-IRON ZUCCHINI BREAD

Zucchini bread is a sweet, quick bread that's perfect for breakfast, brunch, or a snack. Made with fresh zucchini, cinnamon, nutmeg, and cloves, this zucchini bread is best served warm.

Prep Time: 10 minutes| Cook Time: 50 minutes|
Total Time: 1 hour| Servings: 8 slices

Ingredients

- 1 ½ cups (355 ml) shredded zucchini
- 1 ½ cups (355 ml) all-purpose flour
- 1 teaspoon (5 ml) baking soda
- ¼ teaspoon (1 ml) baking powder
- 1 ½ teaspoons (7.5 ml) cinnamon
- ½ teaspoon (2.5 ml) nutmeg
- ¼ teaspoon (1 ml) cloves
- ⅛ teaspoon (.6 ml) fine sea salt
- ½ cup (120 ml) dark brown sugar
- ½ cup (120 ml) granulated white sugar
- ½ cup (120 ml) vegetable oil
- ½ cup (120 ml) coconut milk
- 1 tablespoon (15 ml) apple cider vinegar
- 1 teaspoon (5 ml) vanilla extract

Instructions

1. Turn your oven to 350 °F (175 °C). Grease a 10-inch cast-iron skillet with non-stick cooking spray.
2. Whisk the all-purpose flour, baking powder, baking soda, cinnamon, nutmeg, cloves, and salt in a large bowl.
3. Whisk the brown sugar, white sugar, vegetable oil, coconut milk, apple cider vinegar, and vanilla extract in a separate bowl.
4. Combine the all-purpose flour mixture with the wet ingredients and mix until they are combined.
5. Fold in the zucchini and then pour the bread batter into the prepared pan.
6. Bake the bread batter for 50-60 minutes until a toothpick comes out clean.

7. Let the zucchini bread cool in the skillet for 15 minutes before slicing.
8. Serve and enjoy!

LEMON POPPY SEED SCONES

Crispy edges, soft, flaky interior, and lots of lemon flavor; what could be better? These are not your average lemon poppy seed scones. Featuring rosemary and lavender, these scones are heavenly and delicious.

Prep Time: 10 minutesl Cook Time: 20 minutesl
Total Time: 30 minutesl Servings: 8 scones

Ingredients

For the lemon poppy seed scones

- ⅔ cups (160 ml) canned coconut milk
- ¼ cup (60 ml) freshly squeezed lemon juice
- 2 cups (470 ml) all-purpose flour
- 1 teaspoon (5 ml) fresh rosemary
- 2 tablespoons (30 ml) poppy seeds
- ⅓ cup (80 ml) granulated sugar
- 2 ½ teaspoons (12.5 ml)baking powder
- ½ teaspoons (2.5 ml) salt

- zest of 2 medium lemons
- 6 tablespoons (90 ml) cold vegan butter cut into chunks
- 1 teaspoon (5 ml) lavender extract

Lemon Lavender Glaze

- ½ cup (120 ml) powdered sugar
- 2 tablespoons (30 ml) lemon juice

- 1 teaspoon (5 ml) lavender extract

Instructions

1. Turn your oven to 400 °F (205 °C), then line a large baking sheet with parchment paper.
2. Combine the coconut milk and lemon juice in a small bowl and set it aside for 5 minutes.
3. Whisk the all-purpose flour, rosemary, sugar, poppy seeds, baking powder, salt, and lemon zest in a large bowl until combined.

4. Add the vegan butter to the bowl and, using a pastry cutter or two knives, cut it into the all-purpose flour mixture until it looks like fine crumbs.

5. Stir the lavender extract into the coconut milk mixture. Gradually add the coconut milk mixture and mix until a dough forms. The dough may look dry but mix it until it comes together.

6. Place the dough onto the prepared baking sheet, and with floured hands, form the scone dough into a disc.

7. Cut the scones into 8 scones using a sharp knife. Space the scones 2-inches (5 cm) apart.

8. Bake the scones for 15-20 minutes until the edges are slightly brown.

9. Let them cool on a baking sheet for 5 minutes, then place them on a wire rack to cool completely.

10. To make the lemon lavender glaze, whisk the powdered sugar, lemon juice, and lavender extract in a bowl until smooth.

11. Drizzle the lemon lavender glaze over the lemon poppy seed scones in a zig-zag motion. Let the glaze set for 5 minutes.

12. Serve and enjoy!

COCONUT OAT BREAD

This naturally gluten-free coconut oat bread is moist and delicious. The hardest part of this recipe is waiting for the bread to cool overnight. I know it's hard, but the bread may break in half if you remove it from the pan while it's warm. Luckily this coconut oat bread will be even more delicious on the second day.

Prep Time: 10 minutes| Cook Time: 45 minutes|
Total Time: 55 minutes| Servings: 10 slices

Ingredients

- ½ cup (120 ml) brown sugar-free substitute
- 1 cup (235 ml) unsweetened coconut milk
- ½ cup (120 ml) unsweetened apple sauce
- 1 teaspoon (5 ml) vanilla extract
- 2 ½ cups (590 ml) oat flour
- ¼ cup (60 ml) coconut flour
- ¼ cup (60 ml) ground flaxseed meal
- ¾ teaspoon (4 ml) baking soda

- ½ teaspoon (2.5 ml) baking powder
- ¼ teaspoon (1 ml) salt
- 1 cup (235 ml) shredded coconut
- ¼ cup (60 ml) rolled oats

Instructions

1. Turn your oven to 350 °F (175 °C). Spray a 9 by 5-inch loaf pan with non-stick cooking spray, then line the pan with parchment paper. Spray the paper with non-stick cooking spray.
2. Whisk the brown sugar substitute, coconut milk, apple sauce, and vanilla extract in a large bowl.
3. Add the oat flour, coconut flour, flaxseed meal, baking soda, baking powder, and salt and mix to combine.
4. Fold in the shredded coconut and let the coconut oat flour bread sit for 5 minutes.
5. Pour the bread into the prepared pan and sprinkle the oats on top of the bread.

6. Bake the bread for 40-45 minutes until a toothpick comes out clean.
7. Let the coconut oat bread cool in the pan overnight before slicing.
8. Serve and enjoy!

MAPLE CORNBREAD

Maple and cornbread are a match made in heaven. If you want to make this maple cornbread even better, brush the top of the bread with softened vegan butter. Slather a few tablespoons of maple syrup on top and get ready to eat a slice of heaven.

Prep Time: 10 minutes| Cook Time: 35 minutes|
Total Time: 45 minutes| Servings: 9 slices

Ingredients

- 2 cups (470 ml) almond milk
- 2 teaspoons (10 ml) lemon juice
- ⅓ cup (80 ml) melted vegan butter
- ¼ cup (60 ml) maple syrup
- 1 teaspoon (5 ml) vanilla extract
- 2 cups (470 ml) organic finely ground cornmeal
- 1 cup (235 ml) all-purpose flour
- 2 teaspoons (10 ml) baking powder

- ¼ teaspoon (1 ml) fine sea salt

Instructions

1. Turn your oven to 350 °F (175 °C), then line an 8 by 8 glass or ceramic pan with parchment paper.
2. Whisk the almond milk and lemon juice in a large bowl and let sit for 5 minutes.
3. Whisk in the melted vegan butter, maple syrup, and vanilla extract.
4. Whisk the cornmeal, all-purpose flour, baking powder, and salt in a separate bowl, then whisk the dry ingredients into the wet ingredients.
5. Pour the cornbread into the prepared baking dish and spread it into an even layer.
6. Bake the cornbread for 30-35 minutes until a skewer comes out clean.
7. Let the maple cornbread cool for 5-10 minutes before slicing.
8. Serve and enjoy!

SPICED ORANGE CINNAMON ROLLS

Cinnamon rolls are the best brunch or breakfast food. These easy-to-make cinnamon rolls feature cinnamon, cardamom, and orange juice to jazz things up a bit. The glaze even has orange liqueur in it to further enhance the orange flavor.

Prep Time: 1 hour 20 minutes| Cook Time: 25 minutes| Total Time: 1 hour 45 minutes| Servings: 14 cinnamon rolls

Ingredients

For the dough:

- 2 ¼ (11 ml) teaspoons active dry yeast
- 1 tablespoon (15 ml) brown sugar
- ¼ cup (60 ml) warm water
- 6 tablespoons (90 ml) vegan butter
- 1 cup (235 ml) room temperature almond milk
- ¼ cup (60 ml) room temperature orange juice
- 3 ¼ cups (765 ml) all-purpose flour

- 1 tablespoon (15 ml) orange zest
- ½ teaspoon (2.5 ml) salt

For the filling:

- 2 tablespoons (30 ml) butter melted
- 1 tablespoon (15 ml) cinnamon

- 1 teaspoon (15 ml) cardamom
- ¼ cup (60 ml) brown sugar

For the maple orange glaze:

- 2 cups (470 ml) powdered sugar
- ¼ cup (60 ml) maple syrup
- 1 tablespoon (15 ml) orange liqueur

- 1-2 tablespoons (15 - 30 ml) almond milk

Instructions

1. For the cinnamon roll dough, mix the yeast and sugar in a bowl. Add the water and let the yeast mixture sit for 10 minutes until it is foamy.
2. Whisk the all-purpose flour, orange zest, and salt in a separate bowl.
3. Combine the melted vegan butter, almond milk, and orange juice with the yeast mixture, then stir the yeast orange mixture into the dry ingredients until a shaggy dough forms. Knead the dough for 3 minutes.
4. Grease a bowl with oil, add the cinnamon roll dough to the bowl, cover it with plastic wrap. Let the dough sit for 1 hour until it doubles in size.
5. Whisk the cinnamon, cardamom, and brown sugar in a bowl.
6. Once the dough rises, turn your oven to 350 °F (175 °C).
7. You may have to an additional ¼ cup (60 ml) flour to the dough if it is too sticky.
8. Turn the cinnamon roll dough onto a floured surface and roll it out into a 9 by 14-inch rectangle.
9. Brush the melted vegan butter onto the dough, leaving a 1-inch (2.5 cm) border. Sprinkle the cinnamon brown sugar onto the dough, leaving a 1-inch and roll it into a log.
10. Cut the dough into 9 cinnamon rolls using a sharp knife and place them into a greased baking dish. Place a clean kitchen towel over the cinnamon rolls and let them sit for 30 minutes.
11. Brush the cinnamon rolls with more melted vegan butter if desired and bake them for 20 minutes until they are golden brown.
12. Let the rolls rest for 5 minutes.
13. Whisk the powdered sugar, maple syrup, and orange liqueur in a bowl to make the glaze. Add the almond milk one tablespoon (15 ml) at a time, if necessary, until the glaze is your desired consistency.
14. Drizzle the maple orange glaze over the cinnamon rolls and let sit for 5-10 minutes before digging in.
15. Serve and enjoy!

CHAPTER 3:

CAKES, MUFFINS AND DONUTS

- Vanilla Cake Donuts

- Dutch Raisin Cinnamon Donuts

- Vanilla Cupcakes

- Chocolate Muffins

- Almond Coffeecake

- Olive Oil Tea Loaf Cake

- Blueberry Muffins

- Spiced Nut Cake

- Gluten-Free Maple Sunflower Seed Cake

- Beetroot Chocolate Chip Cake

- Lemon Blueberry Cupcakes

- Apple Coffee Loaf Cake

- Pineapple Upside Down Cake

- Chocolate Cupcakes

- Hazelnut Raisin Poundcake

- Pumpkin Cranberry Muffins

- Pineapple Muffins

VANILLA CAKE DONUTS

The best thing about this vanilla cake donut recipe is that it is super easy to make. It's even made in one bowl! Since these donuts are baked, they have a lighter and fluffier texture than fried donuts.

Prep Time: 10 minutes| Cook Time: 15 minutes|
Total Time: 25 minutes| Servings: 8 donuts

Ingredients

- 1 cup (235 ml) all-purpose flour
- ½ cup (120 ml) granulated white sugar
- 1 teaspoon (5 ml) baking powder
- ¼ teaspoon (1 ml) salt
- ½ cup + 2 tablespoons (150 ml) coconut milk
- 2 tablespoons (30 ml) melted vegan butter
- 1 tablespoon (15 ml) vanilla bean paste

- 2 tablespoons (30 ml) powdered sugar

Instructions

1. Turn your oven to 350 °F (175 °C) and coat a donut pan with 8 cavities with non-stick cooking spray.
2. Whisk the all-purpose flour, sugar, baking powder, and salt in a large bowl.
3. Add the coconut milk, melted vegan butter, and vanilla bean paste to the flour mixture and whisk to combine until the batter has a cake batter consistency. It should not be too thick or too runny.
4. Spoon the donut batter into the prepared pan, filling each cavity 3/4 of the way full. Do not overfill the donut pan.
5. Bake the donuts for 10-15 minutes until they are slightly golden.
6. Let the cake donuts cool in the pan for 2-3 minutes, then place them on a wire rack to cool completely.
7. Place the powdered sugar into a fine-mesh sieve and dust the donuts with the powdered sugar.
8. Serve and enjoy!

DUTCH RAISIN CINNAMON DONUTS

Dutch donuts, also known as Ollie-bollen or Oliebollen, are deep-fried pastries that are made with raisins. Oliebollen are usually served on New Year's Eve. To take these Oliebollen to the next level, you can fill these delicious donuts with berry filling and dust them with powdered sugar.

Prep Time: 2 hours| Cook Time: 8 minutes| Total Time: 2 hours 8 minutes| Servings: 12 doughnuts

Ingredient

- 1 tablespoon (15 ml) ground flaxseed meal
- 3 tablespoons (45 ml) water
- 1 0.6 oz. package of cake yeast (equal to 2 ¼ teaspoons dry yeast/11 ml dry yeast)
- 1 cup (235 ml) lukewarm coconut milk

- 2 ¼ (530 ml) cups all-purpose flour
- 2 teaspoons (10 ml) cinnamon
- 1 teaspoon (5 ml) salt
- ¾ cup (180 ml) raisins
- ¼ cup (60 ml) golden raisins
- 1 Granny Smith apple, peeled, cored, minced
- 4 cups (940 ml) vegetable oil for frying

Instructions

1. Whisk the flaxseed meal and water in a small bowl and set aside for 5 minutes.
2. Break the cake yeast up into smaller pieces, add it to a bowl and stir in the warm coconut milk. Let sit for 5 minutes until the yeast dissolves.
3. Sift the all-purpose flour, cinnamon, and salt into a large bowl.
4. Stir the yeast mixture and flaxseed mixture into the dry ingredients until it is smooth.
5. Stir in the raisins and apples and cover the batter and let sit for 1 hour until it doubles in size.

6. Place the oil into a deep pot and heat it over medium-high heat until it has a temperature of 375 °F (190 °C).
7. Using two metal spoons, shape the batter into scoops of dough and carefully lower them into the hot oil.
8. Fry the donuts for 4 minutes per side until they are golden brown.
9. Drain the Dutch donuts on a paper towel-lined plate.
10. Serve and enjoy!

VANILLA CUPCAKES

There's nothing quite like a soft and fluffy vanilla cupcake. These cupcakes are made with a pinch of cardamom and garnished with a chocolate drizzle and naturally sweet bananas.

Prep Time: 15 minutes| Cook Time: 10 minutes|
Total Time: 25 minutes| Servings: 12 cupcakes

Ingredients

For the cupcakes:

- ½ cup (120 ml) coconut milk
- 1 tablespoon (15 ml) apple cider vinegar
- 1 tablespoon (15 ml) vanilla bean paste
- ⅔ cups (160 ml) pure maple syrup
- 7 tablespoons (105 ml) melted coconut oil
- 2 cups (470 ml) all-purpose flour
- ¼ teaspoon (1 ml) salt
- 1 teaspoon (5 ml) baking powder
- ¼ teaspoon (1 ml) cardamom

For the buttercream frosting:

- 1 cup (235 ml) vegan stick butter, slightly softened
- 3 cups (705 ml) sifted powdered sugar
- 1 teaspoon (5 ml) vanilla bean paste
- 2-3 teaspoons (10 - 15 ml) coconut milk

Toppings

- ¼ cup (60 ml) vegan chocolate sauce
- 1 sliced banana or ½ cup (120 ml) banana chips

Instructions

1. Turn your oven to 350 °F (175 °C), then line a cupcake tin with cupcake liners.
2. To make the vanilla cupcakes, whisk the coconut milk, apple cider vinegar, vanilla bean paste, maple syrup, and coconut oil in a bowl and set aside for 10 minutes.

3. Whisk the all-purpose flour, salt, baking powder, and cardamom in a large bowl. Add the coconut milk mixture and stir until just combined.

4. Add the batter to the prepared pan filling each cup 2/3 of the way up.

5. Bake the cupcakes for 10-12 minutes until a toothpick inserted into the cupcake comes out clean.

6. Let the cupcakes cool in the pan for 5 minutes, then place them onto a wire rack to cool completely.

7. Place the vegan butter into a stand mixer's bowl and cream it using the paddle attachment for 3-5 minutes until the butter is pale and fluffy.

8. Add the vanilla bean paste and mix for 30 seconds until incorporated.

9. Gradually mix in the sifted powdered sugar ½ cup (120 ml) at a time, mixing on low until combined.

10. Increase the mixer's speed to medium and mix the buttercream frosting for 3-5 minutes until it is thick but smooth and fluffy.

11. Add the coconut milk a teaspoon at a time (add the 3rd teaspoon if the frosting is too thick) and mix until combined.

12. Place the buttercream frosting into a piping bag and frost the cupcakes.

13. Garnish the vanilla cupcakes with a drizzle of chocolate sauce and bananas if desired.

14. Serve and enjoy!

CHOCOLATE MUFFINS

You can expect rich, moist, chocolatey flavor when you bite into these chocolate muffins. Made with shredded zucchini, orange zest, and espresso powder, these chocolate muffins are the perfect on-the-go breakfast or snack.

Prep Time: 20 minutes| Cook Time: 20-23 minutes|
Total Time: 40-43 minutes| Servings: 12 muffins

Ingredients

- 1 ½ cups (355 ml) all-purpose flour
- ½ cup (120 ml) unsweetened Dutch-processed cocoa powder
- 1 teaspoon (5 ml) baking powder
- 1 tablespoon (15 ml) orange zest
- 1 teaspoon (5 ml) espresso powder
- ½ teaspoon (2.5 ml) salt
- 1 cup (235 ml) unsweetened oat milk
- ¼ cup (60 ml) melted coconut oil
- 2 tablespoons (30 ml) ground flaxseed meal
- ¾ cup (180 ml) granulated white sugar
- 1 teaspoon (5 ml) vanilla extract
- 1 medium zucchini, shredded
- ¾ cup (180 ml) vegan chocolate chips

Instructions

1. Turn your oven to 350 °F (175 °C), then line a muffin tin with muffin liners.
2. Whisk the all-purpose flour, cocoa powder, baking powder, orange zest, and espresso powder in a large bowl.
3. In a separate bowl, whisk oat milk, coconut oil, flaxseed meal, sugar, and vanilla until smooth.
4. Carefully squeeze the extra water out of the shredded zucchini before folding it into the oat milk mixture.
5. Fold the zucchini oat milk mixture into the dry ingredients.

6. Fold in the chocolate chips and scoop the muffin batter into the prepared pan filling each muffin liner 3/4 full.

7. Bake the muffins for 20-23 minutes until a skewer inserted into a chocolate muffin comes out clean.

8. Let the chocolate muffins cool in the pan for 5 minutes, then place them on a wire rack to cool.

9. Serve and enjoy!

ALMOND COFFEECAKE

The origins of coffee cake are a bit sketchy. It is believed to have originated in Dresden, Germany. However, the Danish had a sweetbread that was served with coffee. Nevertheless, get your cup of coffee ready to go with this gluten-free almond coffee cake.

Prep Time: 15 minutes| Cook Time: 30 minutes|
Total Time: 45 minutes| Servings: 12 slices

Ingredients

For the coffee cake

- ½ cup (120 ml) unsweetened apple sauce
- ½ cup (120 ml) coconut milk
- ⅓ cup (80 ml) melted coconut oil, cooled
- ⅓ cup (80 ml) pure maple syrup
- 1 teaspoon (5 ml) pure vanilla extract
- 2 cups (470 ml) superfine blanched almond flour
- ½ cup (120 ml) tapioca flour

- 1 ½ teaspoons (7.5 ml) baking powder
- ¼ teaspoon (1 ml) sea salt
- 1 cup (235 ml) slivered almonds

For the almond glaze:

- ½ cup (120 ml) powdered sugar
- 1 teaspoon (5 ml) almond extract

- 2 tablespoons (30 ml) almond milk

Instructions

1. Turn your oven to 350 °F (175 °C), coat an 8-inch round springform pan with non-stick cooking spray and line it with parchment paper.
2. Whisk the applesauce, coconut milk, coconut oil, maple syrup, and vanilla extract in a bowl.
3. Whisk the almond flour, tapioca flour, baking powder, and sea salt in a separate bowl.

4. Stir the almond flour mixture into the apple sauce mixture until combined.
5. Pour the batter into the prepared pan and spread it into an even layer.
6. Sprinkle the slivered almonds over the cake and bake it for 35-45 minutes until a skewer comes out clean and coffeecake is golden brown.
7. Let the cake cool on a wire rack for 15 minutes. Loosen the sides of the coffee cake from the pan with a knife and remove the rim from the pan.
8. To make the almond glaze, whisk the powdered sugar, almond extract, and almond milk until smooth.
9. Drizzle the almond glaze over the almond coffee cake.
10. Serve and enjoy!

OLIVE OIL TEA LOAF CAKE

This olive oil tea loaf cake is simple and easy to make and comes together in about an hour. While the cake is sweet, it's not overly sweet, and it's flavored with lots and lots of orange zest. Serve this olive oil tea cake with orange marmalade and a cup of tea for best results.

Prep Time: 10 minutes| Cook Time: 50 minutes|
Total Time: 1 hour| Servings: 12 slices

Ingredients

- 1 ¼ (295 ml) cups all-purpose flour
- ½ teaspoon (2.5 ml) baking powder
- ¼ teaspoon (1 ml) baking soda
- ¼ teaspoon (1 ml) kosher salt
- zest of 2 oranges
- 1 ¼ cups (295 ml) granulated sugar
- ½ cup (120 ml) applesauce
- ¾ cup (180 ml) olive oil
- ½ cup (120 ml) coconut milk
- 1 teaspoon (5 ml) orange extract
- ¼ cup (60 ml) Vin Santo (you can also use another dessert wine)

Ingredients

1. Turn your oven to 350 °F (175 °C). Spray a 9 by 5-inch loaf pan with non-stick cooking spray, then line the pan with parchment paper.
2. Whisk the all-purpose flour, baking powder and soda, salt, and orange zest in a bowl.
3. In a separate bowl, whisk the sugar, apple sauce, olive oil, coconut milk, orange extract, and Vin Santo until combined.
4. Whisk the all-purpose flour mixture into the oil mixture until combined.
5. Add the cake batter to the prepared pan and spread it into an even layer.
6. Bake the cake for 50 minutes until a skewer comes out clean.
7. Let the olive oil tea cake cool in the pan for 5 minutes, then place it onto a wire rack to cool.
8. Serve and enjoy!

BLUEBERRY MUFFINS

These blueberry muffins are loaded with flavor and have the perfect fluffy, yet spongy texture. The secret to getting this perfect texture is simple: do not over mix the muffin batter. The more you mix the blueberry muffin batter, the less powerful the baking powder will be.

Prep Time: 5 minutesl Cook Time: 25 minutesl
Total Time: 30 minutesl Servings: 12 muffins

Ingredients

- 1 cup (235 ml) coconut milk
- ⅓ cup (80 ml) coconut oil
- 2 teaspoons (10 ml) lemon zest
- 1 teaspoon (5 ml) vanilla extract
- 2 cups (470 ml) all-purpose flour
- ¾ cup (180 ml) granulated white sugar
- 2 teaspoons (10 ml) baking powder
- ¼ teaspoon (1 ml) salt
- 1 teaspoon (5 ml) cinnamon
- 2 cups (470 ml) fresh or frozen blueberries

Instructions

1. Turn your oven to 350 °F (175 °C), then line a muffin tin with muffin liners, and lightly spray the liners with non-stick cooking spray.
2. Whisk the coconut milk, coconut oil, lemon zest, and vanilla extract in a bowl and set it aside.
3. Whisk the all-purpose flour, sugar, baking powder, salt, and cinnamon in a separate bowl.
4. Add the coconut milk mixture and mix just until combined.
5. Fold in the blueberries, then carefully and quickly scoop the blueberry muffin batter into the prepared pan filling each cup 3/4 of the way.
6. Bake the muffins for 25 minutes until a toothpick inserted into the muffin comes out clean, and the muffins are golden brown.

7. Allow the blueberry muffins to cool in the pan for 5-10 minutes before placing them on a wire rack to cool.
8. Serve and enjoy!

SPICED NUT CAKE

What's not to love about a spice cake? It is a classic, after all. This spice cake features cinnamon, allspice, nutmeg, and cloves, as well as cashews and walnuts for added texture. Best of all, this spice cake is covered in a deliciously sweet cinnamon buttercream frosting to bring everything together.

Prep Time: 15 minutes| Cook Time: 25 minutes|
Total Time: 40 minutes| Servings: 9 slices

Ingredients

For the spiced nut cake:

- 2 tablespoons (30 ml) ground flaxseed meal
- 6 tablespoons (90 ml) water
- 1 ½ (355 ml) cups all-purpose flour
- 1 teaspoon (5 ml) baking soda
- 1 teaspoon (5 ml) ground cinnamon
- ½ teaspoon (2.5 ml) ground nutmeg
- ¼ teaspoon (1 ml) ground allspice
- ¼ teaspoon (1 ml) ground cloves
- ¼ teaspoon (1 ml) salt
- ¼ cup (60 ml) unsalted vegan butter softened
- ¾ cup (180 ml) granulated white sugar

- 1 cup (235 ml) unsweetened plain applesauce
- 1 teaspoon (5 ml) vanilla extract
- ¼ cup (60 ml) crushed walnuts
- ¼ cup (60 ml) crushed cashews
- ½ cup (120 ml) raisins

For the cinnamon buttercream

- ¼ cup (60 ml) unsalted vegan butter
- 1 cup (235 ml) powdered sugar
- ½ teaspoon (2.5 ml) cinnamon extract
- 1 teaspoon (5 ml) unsweetened coconut milk
- ¼ teaspoon (1 ml) ground cinnamon
- ¼ cup (60 ml) raisins (optional)
- ½ cup (120 ml) walnut halves (optional)

Instructions

1. Turn your oven to 350 °F (175 °C), then coat 2 8-inch round pans with non-stick cooking spray and line them with parchment paper.
2. Whisk the flaxseed meal and water in a small boil and set it aside for 5 minutes.
3. Whisk the all-purpose flour, baking soda, cinnamon, nutmeg, allspice, cloves, and salt until combined.
4. Add the vegan butter, sugar, and flaxseed mixture to a stand mixer's bowl and beat it with the paddle attachment for 2-3 minutes until creamy.
5. Mix in the applesauce and vanilla until incorporated.
6. Gradually add the spiced flour mixture and beat until a thick batter forms.
7. Fold in the walnuts, cashews and raisons, then divide the batter between the prepared pans.
8. Spread the batter into an even layer and bake the cake for 25-30 minutes until a toothpick comes out clean.
9. Let the cake cool in the pan for 10 minutes, then remove it from the pan and remove the parchment paper. Place the cake onto a wire rack to cool completely.
10. To make the cinnamon buttercream, add the butter to a stand mixer's bowl and mix using the paddle attachment until creamy.
11. Mix in the powdered sugar on low. Add the coconut milk and mix until combined.
12. Mix in the cinnamon extract and cinnamon and mix on low speed until combined.
13. Increase the mixer's speed to medium and mix for 2-3 minutes until the cinnamon buttercream frosting is light and fluffy.
14. Frost the spiced nut cake and decorate it with raisins and walnuts if desired.
15. Serve and enjoy!

GLUTEN-FREE MAPLE SUNFLOWER SEED CAKE

Sunflower seeds have an earthy flavor that is even more potent than peanut butter. Inspired to make the most delicious cake, I utilized sunflower seed butter along with maple syrup and gluten-free flours and covered it in a sunflower yellow buttercream frosting.

Prep Time: 20 minutesl Cook Time: 25 minutesl
Total Time: 45 minutesl Servings: 9 slices

Ingredients

For the cake:

- 2 cups (470 ml) unsweetened sunflower seed butter
- ½ cup (120 ml) unsweetened applesauce
- 1 cup (235 ml) coconut milk
- ½ cup (120 ml) maple syrup
- ½ cup (120 ml) coconut sugar
- 1 tablespoon (15 ml) vanilla extract
- 1 cup (235 ml) sweet rice flour
- ½ cup (120 ml) cassava flour
- ¼ cup (60 ml) tapioca starch
- 2 teaspoons (10 ml) cinnamon
- 1 tablespoon (15 ml) baking powder
- ¼ teaspoon (1 ml) salt

For the buttercream frosting:

- 1 cup (235 ml) vegan butter, slightly softened
- 1 teaspoon (5 ml) vanilla extract
- 3 cups (705 ml) sifted powdered sugar
- 2-3 teaspoons (10-15 ml) coconut milk
- 2-3 drops of natural vegan yellow food coloring
- 1 cup (235 ml) blueberries
- 3 raspberries, cut in half

Instructions

1. Turn your oven to 350 °F (175 °C), then coat 2 8-inch round pans with non-stick cooking spray and line them with parchment paper.

2. Whisk the sunflower seed butter, applesauce, coconut milk, maple syrup, coconut sugar, and vanilla extract in a bowl until combined.

3. Whisk the sweet rice flour, cassava flour, tapioca starch, cinnamon, baking powder, and salt in another separate bowl, then fold it into the sunflower seed butter mixture until a smooth batter forms.

4. Divide the cake batter between the prepared pans and spread it into an even layer.

5. Bake the batter for 22-25 minutes until a skewer inserted into the cake comes out clean.

6. Let the cake cool for 10 minutes in the pan.

7. Invert the cakes onto a wire rack, remove the parchment paper, and let the cakes cool completely.

8. To make the buttercream, place the vegan butter into a stand mixer's bowl and cream it using the paddle attachment for 3-5 minutes until the butter is pale and fluffy.

9. Add the vanilla extract and mix for 30 seconds until incorporated.

10. Gradually mix in the sifted powdered sugar ½ cup (120 ml) at a time, mixing on low until combined.

11. Increase the mixer's speed to medium and mix the frosting for 3-5 minutes until thick but smooth and fluffy.

12. Add the yellow food coloring, then add the coconut milk a teaspoon at a time if the frosting is too thick and mix until combined.

13. Frost the sunflower seed cake with the buttercream frosting and garnish it with the blueberries and raspberries.

14. Serve and enjoy!

BEETROOT CHOCOLATE CHIP CAKE

This beetroot chocolate chip cake is incredibly moist and loaded with deliciously healthy beets. Made with dark chocolate and semi-sweet chocolate chips, this cake is the perfect slice of beet heaven.

Prep Time: 20 minutes| Cook Time: 40 minutes|
Total Time: 1 hour | Servings: 12 slices

Ingredients

- 3 tablespoons (45 ml) ground flaxseed meal
- 9 tablespoons (135 ml) water
- 2 large beetroots
- 7 oz. (275 ml/approx. 1 cup + 3 tbsp) 70% dark baking chocolate, chopped thinly
- ½ cup (120 ml) unsalted vegan butter, cut into cubes
- ¼ cup (60 ml) full fat coconut milk
- ¼ cup (60 ml) brown sugar
- 1 cup (235 ml) all-purpose flour
- 1 ½ teaspoons (7.5 ml) baking powder
- ¼ teaspoon (1 ml) fine sea salt
- 1 cup (235 ml) chocolate chips

Instructions

1. Turn your oven to 350 °F (175 °C), then grease a 9-inch cake pan with non-stick cooking spray and line it with parchment.
2. Trim the tops of the beets and peel them. Cut the beets in half and wrap them with aluminum foil.
3. Place the beets into a baking dish or cookie sheet and roast them for 30-45 minutes until they are soft and tender.
4. Remove the roasted beets from the foil and set them aside.
5. Place the dark chocolate and butter into a microwave-safe bowl and heat it in 30-second increments stirring after each burst until the chocolate is melted. Set the melted chocolate butter mixture aside to cool.

6. Whisk the flaxseed meal and water in a small boil and set it aside for 5 minutes.
7. Add the roasted beets to a food processor along with the coconut milk and blend it until it is smooth.
8. Add the flaxseed mixture and brown sugar until combined.
9. Add the melted chocolate butter mixture and whisk until it is smooth and shiny, then add the beetroot mixture and stir to combine.
10. Add the all-purpose flour, baking powder, and salt, and mix to combine.
11. Fold in ¾ cup (180 mL) of the chocolate chips and pour the beetroot chocolate chip cake into the prepared pan.
12. Bake the cake for 20-25 minutes.
13. Let the cake cool in the pan for 10 minutes, then remove from the pan. Place the cake onto a wire rack to cool.
14. Garnish the beetroot chocolate chip cake with the remaining chocolate chips.
15. Serve and enjoy!

LEMON BLUEBERRY CUPCAKES

Lemon and blueberries are the perfect pairing. They complement each other like ice cream and sprinkles. These lemon blueberry cupcakes have a light and fluffy texture, yet they are oh so sweet, and the tart, zesty lemon frosting ties everything together.

Prep Time: 15 minutes| Cook Time: 25 minutes|
Total Time: 40 minutes| Servings: 18 cupcakes

Ingredients

For the lemon cupcakes:

- 2 tablespoons (30 ml) ground flaxseed
- 6 tablespoons (90 ml) water
- 1 cup (235 ml) granulated white sugar
- 1 ¾ (415 ml) cups all-purpose flour
- 1 ½ (7.5 ml) teaspoons baking powder
- 1 teaspoon (5 ml) baking soda
- ½ teaspoon (2.5 ml) salt
- ¼ cup (60 ml) vegan butter, softened
- ⅓ cup (80 ml) cashew yogurt
- ¼ cup (60 ml) unsweetened applesauce
- 1 tablespoon (15 ml) lemon extract
- ⅓ cup (80 ml) unsweetened oat milk
- ⅓ cup (80 ml) freshly squeezed lemon juice
- zest of 1 lemon
- 1 cup (235 ml) fresh blueberries

For the lemon frosting:

- ¾ cup (180 ml) unsalted vegan butter, softened
- 3 cups (705 ml) powdered sugar
- 1 tablespoon (15 ml) lemon extract
- ¼ teaspoon (1 ml) fine sea salt
- 2-3 tablespoons (30-45 ml) unsweetened oat milk
- ½ cup (120 ml) fresh blueberries

Instructions

1. Turn your oven to 350 °F (175 °C), then line two cupcake tins with cupcake liners.
2. Whisk the flaxseed meal and water in a small boil and set it aside for 5 minutes.
3. Add the all-purpose flour, baking powder, baking soda, salt, and sugar to a stand mixer's bowl and mix with the paddle attachment.
4. Add in the softened vegan butter to the dry ingredients and beat on low until it has a sandy texture.
5. Whisk the applesauce, flaxseed and water mixture, cashew yogurt, lemon extract, lemon zest, and lemon juice in a separate bowl.
6. Add the applesauce mixture to the flour-butter mixture and mix until combined.
7. Add the oat milk and mix until the batter is smooth and creamy.
8. Fold in the blueberries and divide the batter between the prepared cupcake tins, filling them up ¾ full.
9. Bake the cupcakes for 20-25 minutes until they are lightly golden, and a skewer inserted in a cupcake comes out clean.
10. Let the cupcakes cool in the pan for 5 minutes, then place them on a wire rack to cool completely.
11. To make the lemon frosting, add the vegan butter and lemon extract to a stand mixer's bowl and mix it with the paddle attachment until it is smooth and creamy.
12. Mix in the powdered sugar a cup at a time until the frosting is thick and creamy.
13. Add the salt and mix to combine.
14. Add the oat milk a tablespoon at a time until the frosting reaches your desired consistency.
15. Place the lemon buttercream frosting into a piping bag and frost the blueberry cupcakes. Garnish the cupcakes with fresh blueberries if desired.
16. Serve and enjoy!

APPLE COFFEE LOAF CAKE

Apples and cinnamon? What could be better? Placing them in a cake together! This apple coffee cake is studded with sweet yet tart apples and warm cinnamon to warm you up any time of the year.

Prep Time: 15 minutesl Cook Time: 50 minutesl
Total Time: 1 hour 5 minutesl Servings: 10 slices

Ingredients

For the apple coffee cake:

- 2 Granny Smith apples, peeled, diced
- 1 ½ teaspoons (7.5 ml) cinnamon
- 1 cup (235 ml) brown sugar
- juice of half a lemon
- 1 ½ cups (355 ml) all-purpose flour
- 1 ½ teaspoons (7.5 ml) baking powder
- 1 teaspoon (5 ml) espresso powder
- ¼ teaspoon (1 ml) salt
- 2 tablespoons (30 ml) apple sauce

- ¼ cup (60 ml) melted vegan butter
- ½ cup (120 ml) oat milk
- 1 teaspoon (5 ml) vanilla extract

For the glaze:

- ½ cup (120 ml) powdered sugar
- 1 teaspoon (5 ml) vanilla extract
- 2 tablespoons (30 ml) grapefruit juice

Instructions

1. Turn your oven to 350 °F (175 °C). Spray a 9 by 5-inch loaf pan with non-stick cooking spray, then line the pan with parchment paper.
2. Place the Granny Smith apples into a bowl and toss them with ¼ cup (60 ml) of brown sugar, cinnamon, and lemon juice.
3. Whisk the apple sauce, melted vegan butter, oat milk, vanilla extract, and the remaining brown sugar in a separate bowl.

4. Whisk the all-purpose flour, baking powder, espresso powder, and salt in another bowl.

5. Add the all-purpose flour dry mixture to the wet mixture and mix just until combined.

6. Fold in ⅔ of the apples, then pour the cake batter into the prepared pan.

7. Add the remaining apples on top of the cake and bake the apple mixture for 40-50 minutes until a skewer inserted into the cake comes out clean.

8. Let the cake cool in the pan for 10 minutes, then remove it from the pan. Place the apple coffee cake on a wire rack to cool.

9. Whisk the powdered sugar, vanilla extract, and grapefruit juice until smooth to make the glaze.

10. Drizzle the glaze over the apple coffee cake.

11. Serve and enjoy!

PINEAPPLE UPSIDE DOWN CAKE

Pineapple upside-down cake played an integral role in many people's childhood. With caramelized pineapples dotted with cherries and a moist and fluffy cake on the bottom, this delicious pineapple upside-down cake will take you back to the past as soon as you taste it.

Prep Time: 20 minutes| Cook Time: 50 minutes|
Total Time: 1 hour 10 minutes| Servings: 8 slices

Ingredients

For the topping:

- 3 tablespoons (45 ml) melted vegan butter
- 6 tablespoons (90 ml) light brown sugar
- 7 canned sliced pineapple rings
- 7 maraschino cherries

For the upside-down pineapple cake:

- 1 ½ cups (355 ml) all-purpose flour
- 1 tablespoon (15 ml) arrowroot flour
- ⅔ cups (160 ml) superfine granulated white sugar
- 1 teaspoon (5 ml) baking powder
- ⅛ teaspoon (.6 ml) fine sea salt
- ⅓ cup (80 ml) room temperature unsweetened oat milk

- ¼ cup (60 ml) pineapple juice
- 3 tablespoons (45 ml) unsweetened cashew yogurt
- ½ cup (120 ml) melted vegan butter
- 2 teaspoons (10 ml) vanilla extract
- 1 teaspoon (5 ml) lemon juice

Instructions

1. Turn your oven to 350 °F (175 °C), then coat an 8-inch round pan with non-stick cooking spray.
2. To make the topping whisk the melted vegan butter and light brown sugar in a bowl. Pour the butter and brown sugar mixture into the prepared pan and spread it into an even layer.

3. Dry the pineapple rings and cherries with a paper towel, then arrange the pineapples on the top of the brown sugar and vegan butter mixture.

4. Place a cherry in the center of each pineapple ring, then place it into the fridge until the cake batter is ready.

5. To make the cake batter, whisk the all-purpose flour, arrowroot flour, sugar, baking powder, and salt in a bowl until combined.

6. Whisk the oat milk, pineapple juice, cashew yogurt, melted vegan butter, vanilla extract, and lemon juice in another bowl.

7. Add the oat milk pineapple juice mixture to the dry flour mixture and stir just until combined.

8. Remove the cake pan from the fridge, pour the batter into the pan, and spread it into an even layer.

9. Bake the pineapple upside-down cake for 50 minutes until a skewer inserted into it comes out clean.

10. Let the cake cool in the pan for 15 minutes, then run a knife around the cake's perimeter to loosen it up.

11. Set a serving dish on top of the cake and carefully invert it onto the dish.

12. Let the pineapple upside-down cake cool completely.

13. Serve and enjoy!

CHOCOLATE CUPCAKES

Chocolate cupcakes are the perfect way to fulfill your chocolate craving. These perfectly sweet and fluffy cupcakes are topped with a decadent chocolate frosting that has a pinch of expresso to take the entire cupcake to the next level.

Prep Time: 10 minutes| Cook Time: 20 minutes|
Total Time: 30 minutes| Servings: 10 cupcakes

Ingredients

For the chocolate cupcakes:

- ¾ cup (180 ml) water
- ¼ cup (60 ml) cashew yogurt
- ¼ cup (60 ml) applesauce
- 2 teaspoons (10 ml) pure vanilla extract
- 1 teaspoon (5 ml) white vinegar
- 1 cup (235 ml) all-purpose flour
- ¼ cup (60 ml) unsweetened cocoa powder
- 2 tablespoons (30 ml) unsweetened Dutch cocoa powder
- ¾ cup (180 ml) granulated white sugar
- ¼ teaspoon (1 ml) salt
- ½ teaspoon (2.5 ml) baking soda

For the chocolate buttercream frosting:

- 1 cup (235 ml) softened vegan butter
- 2 ½ cups (590 ml) powdered sugar
- ½ cup (120 ml) cacao powder
- ½ teaspoon (2.5 ml) espresso powder
- 2–3 tablespoons (30-45 ml) dairy-free milk

Instructions

1. Turn your oven to 350 °F (175 °C), then line a cupcake tin with cupcake liners.
2. To make the vegan cupcakes, whisk the water, cashew yogurt, applesauce, vanilla extract, and white vinegar in a bowl until combined and let it sit for 10 minutes.

3. Sift the all-purpose flour, cocoa powder, Dutch cocoa powder, sugar, salt, and baking soda into a separate bowl.
4. Add the water cashew yogurt mixture to the sifted dry ingredients and mix until smooth.
5. Divide the cupcake batter between each cupcake liner filling each cup 2/3 of the way.
6. Bake the cupcakes for 20 minutes.
7. Let the cupcakes cool in the pan for 10 minutes, then place them onto a wire rack to cool completely.
8. To make the chocolate buttercream frosting, add the vegan butter to a stand mixer's bowl. Beat the vegan butter with the paddle attachment until it is creamy.
9. Sift the cacao powder, espresso powder and powdered sugar into a separate bowl. Add the mixture a cup at a time and mix until a thick frosting forms.
10. Add the oat milk a tablespoon at a time until the chocolate frosting reaches your desired consistency.
11. Place the chocolate frosting into a piping bag and frost the chocolate cupcakes.
12. Serve and enjoy!

HAZELNUT RAISIN POUNDCAKE

Light and fluffy pound cake meets the mellow sweet flavor of hazelnuts. This hazelnut poundcake is fancy and delicious and studded with hazelnuts and raisins in every bite. Best of all, the cake is topped with sliced hazelnuts, so they get nice and toasted in the oven.

Prep Time: 15 minutes| Cook Time: 1 hour| Total Time: 1 hour 15 minutes| Servings: 10 slices

Ingredients

- 1 cup (235 ml) coconut milk
- 1 teaspoon (5 ml) lemon juice
- 3 tablespoons (45 ml) flaxseed meal
- 9 tablespoons (135 ml) water
- ½ cup (120 ml) softened vegan butter
- 1 cup (235 ml) granulated white sugar
- 2 cups (470 ml) all-purpose flour
- 1 tablespoon (15 ml) baking powder
- ¼ teaspoon (1 ml) salt
- 1 tablespoon (15 ml) hazelnut extract
- ⅓ cup (80 ml) raisins
- 1 cup (235 ml) sliced hazelnuts

Instructions

1. Turn your oven to 350 °F (175 °C). Spray a 9 by 5-inch loaf pan with non-stick cooking spray.
2. Mix the coconut milk and lemon juice in a small bowl and set it aside.
3. Whisk the flaxseed meal and water in a small bowl and set it aside for 5 minutes.
4. Add the vegan butter and sugar to a stand mixer's bowl and mix with the paddle attachment for 2-3 minutes until it is light and fluffy.
5. Whisk the all-purpose flour, baking powder, and salt in a bowl until combined.
6. Add ⅓ of the dry flour mixture and mix to combine. Add ½ of the coconut milk and mix to combine. Continue alternating with the dry flour mixture and coconut milk until all of the ingredients are gone.
7. Add the hazelnut extract and mix to combine.

8. Fold in the raisins and half of the hazelnuts, then pour the hazelnut pound cake batter into the prepared pan.

9. Add the remaining hazelnuts on top of the cake.

10. Bake the pound cake for 1 hour until a skewer inserted into the cake comes out clean.

11. Let the hazelnut pound cake cool in the pan for 10 minutes, then place it onto a wire rack to cool.

12. Serve and enjoy!

PUMPKIN CRANBERRY MUFFINS

Ordinary pumpkin muffins get jazzed up with sweet-tart cranberries. Of course, these pumpkin cranberry muffins would not be complete without a healthy helping of warm spices, so we added cinnamon, cardamom, nutmeg, allspice, cloves, and ginger.

Prep Time: 8 minutes| Cook Time: 22 minutes|
Total Time: 30 minutes| Servings: 12 muffins

Ingredients

- 1 15 oz. (1 ⅞ cups/445 ml) can pumpkin puree
- ⅓ cup (80 ml) applesauce
- ½ cup (120 ml) unsweetened oat milk
- 1 ¼ cups (295 ml) light brown sugar
- 1 ¾ cups (415 ml) all-purpose flour
- 1 tablespoon (15 ml) baking powder
- ½ teaspoon (2.5 ml) salt
- 2 teaspoons (10 ml) ground cinnamon
- ½ teaspoon (2.5 ml) ground nutmeg
- ½ teaspoon (2.5 ml) ground ginger

- ¼ teaspoon (1 ml) ground cloves
- ¼ teaspoon (1 ml) allspice
- ⅛ teaspoon (.6 ml) cardamom
- 1 cup (235 ml) cranberries

Instructions

1. Turn your oven to 350 °F (175 °C), then line a muffin tin with muffin liners and lightly spray the liners with non-stick cooking spray.
2. Whisk the pumpkin, applesauce, oat milk, and brown sugar in a large bowl until smooth.
3. Sift the all-purpose flour, baking powder, salt, cinnamon, nutmeg, ginger, cloves, allspice, and cardamom into a large bowl.
4. Add the spiced flour mixture to the pumpkin mixture and mix until combined.
5. Fold in the cranberries, then carefully scoop the pumpkin cranberry muffin batter into the prepared muffin pan filling each cup ¾ of the way full.

6. Bake the muffins for 22-25 minutes until a skewer inserted into a muffin comes out clean.
7. Let the pumpkin cranberry muffins cool in the pan for 10 minutes, then place them on a wire rack to cool completely.
8. Serve and enjoy!

PINEAPPLE MUFFINS

Pineapple muffins are sweet yet refreshing. In addition to this, they are healthy and delicious. While you could eat these muffins for breakfast or brunch, they can also be eaten as a sweet dessert.

Prep Time: 10 minutesl Cook Time: 25 minutesl
Total Time: 35 minutesl Servings: 12 muffins

Ingredients

- 2 cups (470 ml) all-purpose flour
- 2 teaspoons (10 ml) baking powder
- 1 teaspoon (5 ml) ground ginger
- ¼ teaspoon (1 ml) salt
- 1 cup (235 ml) brown sugar
- ½ cup (120 ml) melted vegan butter
- ½ cup (120 ml) applesauce
- 1 cup (235 ml) coconut milk
- 1 teaspoon (5 ml) vanilla extract
- 1 teaspoon (5 ml) pineapple extract
- 1 cup (235 ml) pineapple, chopped

Instructions

1. Turn your oven to 350 °F(175 °C), then coat a muffin tin with non-stick cooking spray.
2. Whisk the all-purpose flour, baking powder, ginger, salt, and sugar in a bowl until combined.
3. Whisk the melted vegan butter, applesauce, coconut milk, vanilla extract, and pineapple extract in a bowl.
4. Whisk the all-purpose flour dry mixture into the melted vegan butter mixture until combined.
5. Fold in the chopped pineapple and scoop it into the prepared pan.
6. Bake the pineapple muffins for 20-25 minutes.
7. Let the pineapple muffins cool in the pan for 5 minutes, then place them on a wire rack to cool.

8. Serve and enjoy!

Notes:

If you are using canned pineapple to make the pineapple muffins, drain it on paper towels before chopping it up.

CHAPTER 4:

TARTS AND PIES

- Apple Pie

- Plum Pie

- Gluten-Free Almond Chocolate Tart

- Strawberry Rhubarb Pie

- Gluten-Free Lime Tarts

- Frangipane Orange Galette

- Lavender Saffron Coconut Crème Brûlée

- Plum Pistachio Tart

APPLE PIE

Apple pie is one of my favorite classics. Sweet, spiced apple pie filling is encased in a buttery, flaky pie crust and baked until golden brown; what could be more delicious than a slice of warm apple pie? Absolutely nothing.

Prep Time: 30 minutesl Cook Time: 40 minutesl
Total Time: 1 hour 10 minutesl Servings: 8 slices

Ingredients

For the pie crust:

- 3 cups (705 ml) all-purpose flour
- 2 tablespoon (30 ml) lemon zest
- 3 tablespoon (45 ml) sugar
- ½ teaspoon (2.5 ml) salt
- 1 cup (235 ml) cold vegan butter, cut into cubes
- 7-8 tablespoons (105-120 ml) ice water

For the apple pie filling:

- 7-8 medium Granny Smith apples, peeled, sliced into ½-inch slices
- 1 tablespoon (15 ml) lemon juice
- ½ cup (120 ml) coconut sugar
- 3 tablespoons (45 ml) all-purpose flour
- 1 teaspoon (5 ml) ground cinnamon
- ½ teaspoon (2.5 ml) anise seed
- ½ teaspoon (2.5 ml) cloves
- ½ teaspoon (2.5 ml) allspice
- 1 teaspoon (5 ml) pure vanilla extract
- 2 tablespoons (30 ml) vegan butter
- 2 tablespoons (30 ml) coconut milk

Instructions

1. Place the all-purpose flour, lemon zest, sugar, and salt in a food processor outfitted with the "S" blade and pulse it a few times to combine.
2. Add the vegan butter and pulse it for 10 seconds until it looks like coarse breadcrumbs.

3. Add 6 tablespoons (90 ml) of ice water while the food processor is still running. The pie crust should clump together. If it doesn't, add the remaining tablespoons of ice water one at a time and process until it comes together.

4. Place the pie crust onto a lightly floured surface, divide it in half, and shape the halves into a ball.

5. Wrap each half of the pie crust with plastic wrap and chill it in the fridge while you make the pie filling.

6. Place the Granny Smith apples into a saucepan and add the lemon juice, coconut sugar, all-purpose flour, cinnamon, anise seed, cloves, allspice, and vanilla extract and stir to combine to make the apple pie filling.

7. Cook the filling over medium-high heat for 10-15 minutes, often stirring, until the apples start to soften.

8. Remove the apple pie filling from the heat and set it aside.

9. Turn your oven to 350 °F (175 °C).

10. Remove the pie crusts from the refrigerator and roll a disc into a 12-inch circle and carefully place it into a pie plate.

11. Carefully push the pie crust flush against the pie plate and trim off any excess crust.

12. Pour the slightly cooled apple pie filling on top of the pie crust and spread it into an even layer. Dot the filling with the vegan butter

13. Roll out the second pie crust into a 12-inch circle and drape it over the pie crust.

14. Trim the excess pie crust and seal the edges of the pie crust by crimping it your fingers.

15. Cut a few impressions into the apple pie to prevent it from exploding in the oven, then brush the apple pie with the coconut milk.

16. Bake the apple pie for 40 minutes until it is golden brown.

17. Let the apple pie cool for 30 minutes.

18. Serve and enjoy!

PLUM PIE

This plum pie is made of a flaky pie crust and a sweet plum filling that's made with cinnamon, ginger, brown sugar, maple syrup, and a secret ingredient, black pepper. Who knew maple syrup and black pepper would bring the best out of plums?

Prep Time: 30 minutes| Cook Time: 45 minutes|
Total Time: 1 hour 15 minutes| Servings: 8 slices

Ingredients

For the crust:

- 1 ¾ cups (415 ml) all-purpose flour
- ¼ teaspoon (1 ml) salt
- ¼ teaspoon (1 ml) cinnamon
- 1 teaspoon (5 ml) lemon zest
- 2 tablespoons (30 ml) brown sugar
- 7 ounces (⅞ cup/205 ml) vegan butter
- 6 tablespoons (90 ml) olive oil
- 6 tablespoons (90 ml) cold water

For the filling:

- 1 pound plums, sliced (approx. 6-8 plums/2 ½ cups/585 ml)
- 2 tablespoons (30 ml) maple syrup
- ¼ teaspoon (1 ml) black pepper
- 2 teaspoons (10 ml) cinnamon
- ½ teaspoon (2.5 ml) ginger
- ½ teaspoon (2.5 ml) allspice
- 2 tablespoons (30 ml) brown sugar
- juice of ½ lemon
- 2 tablespoons (30 ml) cornstarch
- 2 tablespoons (30 ml) powdered sugar

Instructions

1. To make the crust, add the all-purpose flour, salt, cinnamon, lemon zest, brown sugar, and vegan butter to a food processor. Pulse until it looks like coarse crumbs.
2. Whisk the olive oil and water in a small bowl and gradually add it to the flour-butter mixture, and pulse until a dough starts to form.

3. Divide the pie crust into 2 pieces and flatten them into discs.
4. Wrap the pie crusts with plastic wrap and refrigerate for 30 minutes.
5. Turn your oven to 350 °F (175 °C).
6. Roll out one pie crust into a 12-inch circle and place it in a pie plate.
7. Place the plums, maple syrup, black pepper, cinnamon, ginger, allspice, brown sugar, lemon juice, and cornstarch and toss to combine.
8. Add the plums to the bottom pie crust and set it aside.
9. Roll out the second pie crust and use a circle cookie cutter and the bottom of a piping tip to cut circles in the pie crust.
10. Place the pie crust over the plum filling, trim the excess dough away from the pie plate and seal the edges of the crust.
11. Bake the pie for 40-45 minutes until it is golden brown.
12. Let the plum pie sit for 30 minutes, then dust it with powdered sugar if desired.
13. Serve and enjoy!

GLUTEN-FREE ALMOND CHOCOLATE TART

There is nothing more elegant than a chocolate tart. Although it seems intimidating, this chocolate tart is pretty easy to make. It features a chewy nut crust and creamy chocolate ganache. Topped with fresh raspberries and almonds, this tart is stunningly delicious.

Prep Time: 30 minutes| Cook Time: 10 minutes| Total Time: 40 minutes| Servings: 8 slices

Ingredients

For the nut crust:

- 1 cup (235 ml) of dates, soaked in boiled water for 15 minutes and drained
- 1 cup (235 ml) almond flour
- 1 teaspoon (5 ml) cinnamon
- ¼ teaspoon (1 ml) nutmeg
- 1 cup (235 ml) whole pecans
- 1 cup (235 ml) old fashioned oats
- 2 tablespoons (30 ml) coconut oil

For the chocolate filling:

- 6 oz. (1 cup/235 ml) bittersweet chocolate, finely chopped
- 6 oz. (1 cup/235 ml) semi-sweet chocolate, finely chopped
- 1 cup (235 ml) full-fat coconut milk

- 1 tablespoon (15 ml) orange zest
- 1 teaspoon (5 ml) vanilla extract
- 1 tablespoon (15 ml) coffee extract
- ¼ teaspoon (1ml) fine sea salt

For the toppings:

- ½ cup (120 ml) toasted slivered almonds
- 8 raspberries

Instructions

1. To make the nut crust add the dates, almond flour, cinnamon, nutmeg, pecans, oats, and coconut oil to a food processor. Pulse until the nut mixture has a sticky yet crumb-like mixture forms.
2. If the nut crust does not come together, add 2 tablespoons (30 ml) of water and mix until a sticky mixture comes together.
3. Add the nut crust into a square tart tin and spread it into an even layer. Make sure the pie crust reaches up the edges of the tart pan. Set the nut crust aside.
4. To make the chocolate filling, add the chopped bittersweet and semi-sweet chocolate into a bowl and set it aside.
5. Add the coconut milk and orange zest to a saucepan set it over medium-low heat, and let the coconut milk come to a simmer.
6. Pour the coconut milk over the chopped chocolate and let it sit for 2 minutes.
7. Stir the chocolate coconut milk mixture until it is smooth and creamy, then whisk in the vanilla extract, coffee extract, and sea salt.
8. Pour the chocolate ganache filling into the nut crust, let it cool slightly, then cover the tart and chill it in the fridge 3 hours or overnight until it is set.
9. Add the toasted almonds and raspberries to the chocolate tart.
10. Serve and enjoy!

STRAWBERRY RHUBARB PIE

Strawberries and rhubarb belong together like vegan ice cream and pie. Baked inside a flaky buttery crust, the tart flavor of rhubarb and sweet flavor of strawberries work together to create an explosion of irresistible flavor in your mouth.

Prep Time: 40 minutes| Cook Time: 50 minutes|
Total Time: 1 hour 30 minutes| Servings: 8 slices

Ingredients

For the pie crust:

- 2 ½ cups (590 ml) all-purpose flour
- ¼ teaspoon (1 ml) cardamom
- ¼ teaspoon (1 ml) ginger
- 3 tablespoons (45 ml) sugar
- ½ teaspoon (2.5 ml) salt
- 1 cup + 2 tablespoons (235 ml + 30 ml) cold vegan butter
- 3-5 tablespoons (45-75 ml) ice water

For the strawberry rhubarb filling:

- 3 cups (705 ml) sliced strawberries
- 5-6 rhubarb stalks (about 3 cups/705 ml), sliced
- ½ cup (120 ml) granulated sugar
- ¼ cup (60 ml) cornstarch
- 1 tablespoon (15 ml) lemon juice
- 1 teaspoon (5 ml) vanilla extract
- ¼ teaspoon (1 ml) salt
- ¾ teaspoon (4 ml) cardamon
- ¾ teaspoon (4 ml) ginger
- 2 tablespoons (30 ml) vegan butter
- 2 tablespoons (30 ml) coconut milk

Instructions

1. Spray a 9-inch pie pan with non-stick cooking spray and set it aside.
2. Whisk to combine the all-purpose flour, cardamom, ginger, sugar, and salt in a bowl.
3. Add the vegan butter to the bowl and, using a pastry cutter or two knives, cut it into the all-purpose flour mixture until it looks like pea-sized crumbs.

4. Pour a tablespoon (15 ml) of ice water over the butter-flour mixture and mix until a dough forms. Add more ice water to the butter-flour mixture one tablespoon (15 ml) at a time if necessary and mix until a dough forms.

5. Wrap the pie crust in plastic wrap and chill it in the fridge for 30 minutes.

6. Cut the pie crust in half and roll out each piece of dough between 2 sheets of parchment paper until it is 1/8-inches in thickness and 12-inches in diameter.

7. Place the bottom crust into the prepared pie plate and refrigerate it until the strawberry rhubarb filling is ready.

8. Turn your oven to 400 °F (205 °C).

9. Add the strawberries, rhubarb, sugar, cornstarch, lemon juice, vanilla extract, salt, cardamom, and ginger, in a bowl and toss to combine.

10. Place the strawberry rhubarb filling into the prepared pie crust and dot it with butter.

11. Add the top crust to the strawberry rhubarb pie, trim the excess pie crust, and seal the edges of the pie.

12. Cut a few impressions into the pie crust and brush the strawberry rhubarb pie with the coconut milk.

13. Bake the pie for 25 minutes, then decrease the oven's temperature to 350 °F (175 °C) and bake it for another 25 minutes until the pie is golden brown.

14. Let the strawberry rhubarb pie cool completely.

15. Serve and enjoy!

GLUTEN-FREE LIME TARTS

Limes have a tart, yet slightly sweet flavor that is perfect for making tarts. These lime tarts are no-bake, gluten-free, and paleo, so get ready to indulge in a healthy lime tart with a crunchy crust and creamy lime filling.

Prep Time: 30 minutes| Cook Time: 0 minutes|
Total Time: 30 minutes| Servings: 3 mini tarts

Ingredients

For the nut crust:

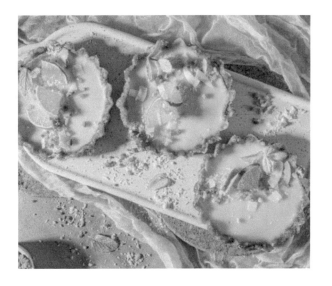

- ½ cup (120 ml) almond flour
- ½ cup (120 ml) walnut flour
- 4 pitted Medjool dates
- 2 tablespoons (30 ml) coconut oil
- ¼ teaspoon (1 ml) fine sea salt
- 2 tablespoons (30 ml) fresh lime juice
- 1 teaspoon (5 ml) lime zest

For the lime filling:

- 1 cup (235 ml) raw cashews, soaked in cold water for 4 hours or overnight
- ½ cup (120 ml) fresh lime juice
- ⅓ cup (80 ml) coconut oil
- ¼ cup (60 ml) coconut milk
- ¼ cup (60 ml) agave nectar
- 1 tablespoon (15 ml) lime zest
- 1 teaspoon (5 ml) vanilla extract
- ¼ teaspoon (1 ml) fine sea salt

For the toppings:

- ¼ cup (60 ml) mint leaves
- ¼ cup (60 ml) crushed almonds
- ¼ cup (60 ml) shaved coconut
- 1 lime, cut into ¼-inch (.6 cm) slices, then quartered

Instructions

1. Grease 3, 4-inch tart pans with coconut oil and set them aside.
2. Add the almond flour, walnut flour, Medjool dates, coconut oil, sea salt, lime juice and zest to a food processor. Pulse until the nut crust sticks together.
3. Divide the nut crust between the prepared pans and spread them into an even layer, making sure to press the crust into the sides of the tart pans.
4. Add the cashews, key lime juice, coconut oil, coconut milk, agave nectar, lime zest, vanilla extract, and fine sea salt to a blender and blend until it has a silky smooth texture.
5. Pour the lime filling into the nut crusts and refrigerate the lime tart for at least 2 hours until it is set.
6. Garnish the lime tarts with mint, almond, coconut, and lime slices if desired.
7. Serve and enjoy!

FRANGIPANE ORANGE GALETTE

Galettes are French tarts that, unlike pie crusts, are very forgiving. The best part is since galettes are rustic, there's no need to make the perfect tart. The beauty of galettes is their rusticness. To make this tart, a frangipane filling is spread onto a flaky galette crust, and oranges are arranged on top of it; then the galette is baked to perfection.

Prep Time: 30 minutes| Cook Time: 25 minutes|
Total Time: 55 minutes| Servings: 6 slices

Ingredients

For the galette crust:

- 2 cups (470 ml) all-purpose flour
- ½ teaspoon (2.5 ml) fine sea salt
- ⅛ teaspoon (.6 ml) mace
- 3 tablespoons (45 ml) superfine granulated sugar
- ⅔ cups (160 ml) cold vegan butter
- 4-6 tablespoons (60-90 ml) ice water

For the orange filling:

- ½ cup (120 ml) almond flour
- ¼ cup (60 ml) brown sugar
- ⅓ cup (80 ml) melted vegan butter
- 1 teaspoon (5 ml) arrowroot flour
- 1 teaspoon (5 ml) ground mace
- ½ teaspoon (2.5 ml) ground cinnamon
- 5 oranges, peeled, cut into ½-inch rings

Instructions

1. Whisk the all-purpose flour, salt, sugar, and mace in a bowl.
2. Add the vegan butter to the bowl and, using a pastry cutter or two knives, cut it into the all-purpose flour mixture until it looks like pea-sized crumbs.

3. Pour 4 tablespoons (60 ml) of water over the flour-butter mixture and mix until a slightly smooth wet dough forms. Add the remaining 2 tablespoons (30 ml) of water one at a time if the dough is a little dry.

4. Shape the galette dough into a flat round, cover it with plastic wrap, and chill it in the fridge for 30 minutes.

5. Turn your oven to 375 °F (190 °C).

6. Mix the almond flour, brown sugar, melted vegan butter, arrowroot flour, mace, and cinnamon in a bowl until combined.

7. Place the galette dough between 2 sheets of parchment paper and roll it into a 12-inch circle that is ¼-inch (.6 cm) in thickness.

8. Remove the top parchment and place the galette crust onto a cookie sheet.

9. Spread the orange filling over the galette crust, leaving a 1-inch border around the perimeter of the crust.

10. Layer the oranges on top of the filling and fold the edges of the crust over.

11. Bake the galette for 20-25 minutes until the crust is crispy and golden brown.

12. Let the orange galette cool for 20 minutes to firm up.

13. Serve and enjoy!

LAVENDER SAFFRON COCONUT CRÈME BRÛLÉE

Crème Brûlée also known as burnt cream is a dessert that has a rich and creamy base and a sugary caramelized top. In this variety the Crème Brûlée base is infused with delicious lavender and saffron. This lavender saffron coconut Crème Brûlée is an elegant grand finale to any meal.

Prep Time: 5 minutes| Cook Time: 10 minutes|
Total Time: 15 minutes| Servings: 3

Ingredients

For the Crème Brûlée:

- 1 cup (235 ml) coconut cream
- 1 ½ cups (355 ml) coconut milk
- ¼ cup (60 ml) cornstarch
- ¼ cup (60 ml) granulated white sugar
- 1 tablespoon (15 ml) lavender extract
- 1 teaspoon (5 ml) saffron threads
- ¼ teaspoon (1 ml) fine sea salt

For the caramelized top:

- 3 tablespoons (45 ml) sugar

Instructions

1. Add the coconut cream, coconut milk, and cornstarch to a medium saucepan and whisk until the cornstarch is dissolved.
2. Stir in the sugar, lavender extract, saffron threads, and sea salt, and heat the batter over medium-high heat, periodically stirring until it comes to a boil.
3. Turn the flame to medium-low and cook the batter for 5-6 minutes, constantly stirring until it thickens and has a custard consistency.
4. Divide the Crème Brûlée batter between 3 ramekins, let them cool for 30 minutes at room temperature, then wrap them with plastic wrap and chill them for 4 hours.
5. To make the caramelized top, add a tablespoon of sugar to the top of each Crème Brûlée and spread it into an even layer.

6. With a blow torch, burn the granulated sugar evenly until it has a beautiful glossy caramelized color.
7. Serve and enjoy immediately!

PLUM PISTACHIO TART

Plums and pistachios are an unlikely pairing. However, they work very well in this dish. This plum pistachio tart is easy to make and super delicious. Best of all, your loved ones will never know you cheated by using vegan puff pastry!

Prep Time: 10 minutes| Cook Time: 35 minutes|
Total Time: 45 minutes| Servings: 4 mini tarts

Ingredients

- 1 sheet vegan puff pastry sheet thawed
- 6 red plums, thinly sliced
- 4 tablespoons (60 ml) brown sugar
- 1 teaspoon (5 ml) ground cinnamon
- 1 teaspoon (5 ml) ground ginger
- ½ cup (120 ml) pistachios, chopped

Instructions

1. Turn your oven to 375 °F (190 °C).
2. Coat a 14 by 4.5-inch oblong tart pan with non-stick spray.
3. Place the puff pastry into the pan and press it into the bottom and sides of the tart pan, then use a paring knife to trim the excess puff pastry from the pan.
4. With a fork, prick the puff pastry to prevent it from rising too much.
5. Place the plums into a bowl and toss with the brown sugar, cinnamon, and ginger.
6. Arrange the plums on top of the puff pastry and top with the pistachios.
7. Bake the tart for 30-35 minutes until the crust is crispy and golden brown.
8. Let the plum pistachio tart cool for 15 minutes before slicing.
9. Serve and enjoy!

CONCLUSION

There are several reasons why people commit to a vegan diet. For example, it could be because of environmental issues or health issues. Nevertheless, you should not starve yourself from eating baked goods because you think they are not vegan. As this cookbook has shown you, there are delicious vegan baked goods that are free of animal products. Truthfully, it's just a matter of making a grocery run and getting to work in the kitchen.

Moreover, you do not have to run out to your local bakery whenever you crave a vegan cake or tart. You can make your own vegan baked goods at home. Not only will they be even more delicious, but you can control what goes into the product, so there are no hidden non-vegan ingredients in your baked goods. Furthermore, it will foster an appreciation for baking since you will be enjoying the delicious fruits of your labor.

Unfortunately, most people are unaware that non-vegan foods can be turned into vegan foods. Furthermore, they believe that the flavor of the food will be diminished. However, now that you've got 50 new baking recipes in your arsenal, you can prove the critics wrong - one baked good at a time.

Made in United States
Troutdale, OR
02/22/2024

17885060R00066